EVERY CHILD INCLUDED

EVERY CHILD INCLUDED

Rona Tutt

Paul Chapman Publishing

The Association for all School Leaders

Paul Chapman Publishing
A SAGE Publications Company
1 Oliver's Yard
55 City Road
London EC1Y 1SP

SAGE Publications Inc.
2455 Teller Road
Thousand Oaks, California 91320

SAGE Publications India Pvt Ltd
B1/I1 Mohan Cooperative Industrial Area
Mathura Road
New Delhi 110 044

SAGE Publications Asia-Pacific Pte Ltd
33 Pekin Street # 02-01
Far East Square
Singapore 048763

Library of Congress Control Number: 2007921184

A catalogue record for this book is available from the British Library

ISBN- 978-1-4129-4488-5
ISBN- 978-1-4129-4489-2 (pbk)

Typeset by Pantek Arts Ltd, Maidstone, Kent
Printed in Great Britain by Cromwell Press Ltd, Trowbridge, Wiltshire
Printed on paper from sustainable resources

C ONTENTS

The Association for all School Leaders

With a membership of over 28,000, the National Association of Head Teachers is the largest organization of its kind in Europe. Representing headteachers, principals, deputies, vice-principals and assistant headteachers, it has provided over a century of dedicated support to its members. The union speaks with authority and strength on educational issues covering early years, primary, secondary and special sectors.

National Association of Head Teachers
1 Heath Square, Boltro Road, Haywards Heath, West Sussex, RH16 1BL
Tel: +44 1444 472472; email: info@naht.org.uk; website: www.naht.org.uk

Rona Tutt has taught students with SEN in state and independent, residential and day, mainstream and special schools. Trained orginally as a teacher of the deaf, for several years she was the head teacher of Woolgrove School in Hertfordshire, a school for pupils who have moderate learning difficulties (MLD). She established the Local Authority's first provision for pupils with autistic spectrum disorders (ASD) within the school.

In March 2003, Rona was the winner of the Leadership in Teaching Award. In February 2004, she received an OBE for her services to special needs education. From 2004 until 2005, she was President of the National Association of Head Teachers (NAHT), the first head of a special school to reach this position. She continues to work for them as an SEN consultant.

Rona writes on a number of educational issues and is much in demand as a speaker. She has addressed a range of different audiences, including parents and carers, school governors and professionals from across education, health and social services. She has spoken at conferences in America, Australia and Canada. She is undertaking postdoctoral research into co-existing and overlapping disorders at the University of Hertfordshire.

Rona is Chair of Governors at Heathlands School in St Albans, which caters for severely and profoundly deaf children, and Vice Chair of Governors at The Valley School in Stevenage, which is for secondary pupils with MLD and ASD.

DEDICATION

I would like to dedicate this book to the pupils, staff, governors and parents of Woolgrove School with whom I spent so many happy and productive years.

I know the staff will continue to show the same compassion and commitment to present and future pupils, as they have in the past.

ACKNOWLEDGEMENTS

The heart of this book is based on a series of visits I made to schools that represented different parts of the continuum of provision for pupils who have special educational needs – from a children's centre to an academy, from a first school to a girls' secondary school, and from a large generic special school in Wales to a group of special schools in Northern Ireland. I would like to thank each one of these schools, and all those featured in the case studies, for the warmth of their welcome, for making time for me amid the pressures of their school day, and for ensuring that I left with a feeling of elation about what they were achieving for pupils who have special educational needs.

The schools visited were:

The Thomas Coram Centre for Children and Families
Tuckswood Community First School
Tolworth Girls' School and Centre for Continuing Education
The City Academy, Bristol
Baytree School
Priestley Smith School
Wilson Stuart School
Oakwood School and Assessment Unit
Glenveagh School
Harberton School
Fleming Fulton School
St Christopher's School, Wrexham
Ysgol Plas Brondyffryn
Heathlands School
The Ashley School
Sunfield School

Others featured include:

Colnbrook School
Woolgrove School
The New Rush Hall Group
The Compass Centre
N. Lincs SEN Support Service
Hertfordshire's Primary Support Bases
Rotherham's Integrated SEN and Disability Service

I would also like to thank the individuals who guided my footsteps to the right schools, including Anna Brychan (Director, NAHT, Wales), Claire Dorer (Chief Executive, NASS), Deryn Harvey (Director, Innovation Unit, DfES), David Ryan, (SEN Advisor, Belfast), Toby Salt (Strategic Director, NCSL), Gwen Williams, (former NAHT Council Member, Wales).

Also, my thanks to Peter Gray for permission to use figure 4.4 and to Lorraine Petersen, Chief Executive, for permission to use three poems from the NASEN publication, *Like everyone else* … Figure 6.1 is Parliamentary copyright material and is reproduced with permission of the Controller of Her Majesty's Stationery Office on behalf of Parliament.

My final thanks go to:

Members of the NAHT SEN Committee, for their practical support and encouragement throughout the project.

To my colleague, former President of NASEN, Tricia Barthorpe, for her words of great wisdom and reassurance at every turn.

And, finally, to my long-suffering husband, David, who, despite my increasing neglect of him, took over the household chores and acted as my technical support, when the idiosyncrasies of my new laptop defeated me.

It may be my name on the front of the book, but all the people mentioned above enabled me to turn an idea into a reality, aided and abetted, of course, by Jude Bowen, Senior Commissioning Editor and Katie Metzler, Assistant Editor at Paul Chapman Publishing SAGE Publications, who both showed exemplary patience in dealing with the concerns of a first-time author.

HOW TO USE THIS BOOK

This book aims to track the move to creating a more flexible continuum of provision for pupils with special educational needs (SEN), and, at the same time, to comment on the complementary agenda that is unfolding around 'Every Child Matters'.

The book considers developments in the provision for pupils with SEN, from the various types of support available in mainstream schools to 52 weekly placements in specialist settings. There has been a significant shift from thinking in terms of two discrete sectors, mainstream and special, to schools and SEN services working together to support the diversity of needs present in today's classrooms.

The format for most of the chapters is similar:

■ The main points of the chapter are highlighted at the beginning

■ 'Questions for reflection', are given near the start of the chapter, which link with the 'Final thoughts' at the end

■ 'Case studies' to demonstrate current developments in schools

■ 'Successful strategies' and 'Points to ponder' are provided after each case study

■ Most chapters end with 'Ten tips for best practice'

Although some readers may prefer to start by dipping into the chapters that interest them most, the contents are laid out to show the range of specialist provision, starting with case studies of mainstream provision in Chapter 2, special schools in Chapter 3, and residential provision in Chapter 4. Chapter 5 looks at the growing range of SEN support services and the final chapter draws together the themes that have arisen throughout the book and uses them to suggest ways forward.

Several chapters include photocopiable resources. Some of these are pro formas, while others show work developed by schools and will need adapting, but may prove useful as a starting point for discussion, or for producing similar versions that are applicable to schools' own situations.

I hope the book will convey something of the creative energy to be found in so many of our schools, as they join forces with each other, and provide a range of services, to make sure every child really does feel that he or she is included somewhere along the continuum of provision – a continuum that is expanding all the time to meet the needs of those who deserve our support, as they strive to overcome the obstacles that otherwise stand in the way of their path to progress.

DISABILITY

Do you know what it's like to
Lose your sight?

Invisible things are to me, but
Not to you.

So you think you know what it's
Like, you still have your sight

Able I am! Just like you.

Braille is a new language for
You and me

I will have a full life of fun and
Joy
Like you I can work too.

I look forward to the fun things
In life.
Treats that I love just like you!

You and I are just alike, apart
From the fact I'm losing my sight.

Rhys Wilson, 13 years old
Sir Thomas Picton School
Haverfordwest, Pembrokeshire

'Like everyone else ...'
A collection of poems on 'inclusion'
NASEN 2006.

CHAPTER 1

The Inclusion and Every Child Matters agendas

This chapter sets the scene for the rest of the book. It explains how:

- the inclusion debate has developed to encompass the notion of all schools being part of a flexible continuum of provision

- the Every Child Matters agenda is unfolding alongside inclusion

- the chapters in the book are set out to illustrate how an inclusive education service is being developed across schools and services

The convoluted path of inclusion

After many years of argument about what inclusion should mean with regard to pupils who have special educational needs, there is a growing consensus about how the concept of inclusion should be defined. In the past, the debate centred almost entirely around a small percentage of pupils with the most significant needs and where their education should take place. This is 'inclusion' in the narrow sense of 'placement'. After a quarter of a century of unproductive and heated argument, there is, at last, widespread agreement that inclusion is not about a place at all, but describes a process.

All schools need to work hard at making pupils feel they are part of the school community and have something to contribute. This is particularly necessary where, for a variety of reasons, including having special educational needs, pupils may find it harder to be accepted by their peers and appreciated for what they have to offer. Any type of school may or may not be an inclusive school, depending on the ethos of the school, and how staff try to accommodate and value all pupils. Special schools, in common with mainstream schools, have encountered the challenges of being asked to take on pupils with needs that are outside their experience, and have had to find ways of making sure the school adapts to provide for such pupils, as well as it does for the rest of its population. This means that special schools do not stand outside inclusion, as is sometimes implied; they are part of it.

The concept of inclusion has moved on from meaning all pupils being included in mainstream schools to the much more productive idea of all schools working together as part of an inclusive education service. Nor is it only schools that are part of inclusion. Advisory and support services too have a significant role to play in supporting pupils with special educational needs, wherever they are being educated.

The lengthy debate around the meaning of inclusion has hindered the development of a coherent education service, within which there is agreement about how to meet the whole range of needs, from the vast majority of pupils who require varying levels of support in mainstream schools, right through to those whose needs are so severe that a 52-week placement may be considered. Instead, local authorities and individual schools have been inclined to devise their own ways forward, outside any national framework.

Examples from across the range of provision are given in the following chapters. The case studies have been chosen to illustrate some of the many ways in which schools, both mainstream and special, as well as advisory and support services, are moving forward in new ways to embrace the concept of working together to meet the needs of all pupils. A range of innovative practices is emerging, that illustrate some of the many and varied ways that pupils with special educational needs are being included in a very real sense. An added impetus to this work has been the unfolding of the Every Child Matters agenda, with its emphasis on placing children and their individual needs at the heart of what schools do, rather than thinking in terms of what is most convenient for the institution.

Terminology and SEN

The term 'special educational needs' was used by the committee set up in the 1970s, under the chairmanship of Mary Warnock, to look at the education of 'handicapped children and young people.' The term was used widely on its own until the Special Educational Needs and Disability Act of 2001 brought the two terms 'SEN' and 'Disability' together. Although the expressions are not synonymous, there is considerable overlap between them. The Disability Rights Commission's *Code of Practice for Schools* (2002) explains that:

> Pupils may have either a disability or special educational needs or both. The SEN framework is designed to make the provision to meet special educational needs. The disability discrimination duties, as they relate to schools, are designed to prevent discrimination against disabled children in their access to education. (Paragraph 4.10)

Further shifts in terminology can be detected through recent reports from Ofsted:

- *Special educational needs in the mainstream* (2003)

- *Special educational needs and disability: towards inclusive schools* (2004)

- *Inclusion: does it matter where pupils are taught? Provision and outcomes in different settings for pupils with learning difficulties and disabilities* (2006)

In the last of these three reports, the term 'SEN' or 'SEN and Disability' is replaced with 'Learning Difficulties and Disabilities' (LDD). The explanation for this is given in the report itself:

> The term LDD is used to cross the professional boundaries between education, health and social services and to incorporate a common language for 0–19 year olds. In the context of this report, it replaces the term special educational needs. (Page 21)

Ofsted has a valid point. With the roll out of Every Child Matters, a common language across services, particularly education, health and social care, is much needed. The difficulty is that the term 'SEN and Disability' is enshrined in law and the DfES will continue to use it. For the sake of simplicity, 'SEN' will be used throughout this book.

Questions for reflection

- What is your own view of inclusion?

- Do you think it is time to replace the word 'inclusion' in the context of special educational needs?

- Does the term 'SEN' itself need replacing, and if so, have you any suggestions as to what should be put in its place?

The background to the inclusion and Every Child Matters agendas

In schools, there is often a feeling of a lack of cohesion between government policies and a sense of despair when some of them seem contradictory; for example, the need to raise standards for all can be accepted as a general principle, but the way to set about achieving this has caused much anxiety, not least for those concerned with the progress of pupils with SEN. Personalising the curriculum and focusing on the needs of every individual, sits uncomfortably with the notion that all pupils of the same age should be tested on the same day. Performance tables may have been renamed 'Achievement and Attainment Tables,' but they still measure the attainments of some, rather than recognising the achievements of all pupils, whatever the level they have reached.

However, two agendas that do sit comfortably together are those of inclusion and Every Child Matters (ECM). To understand how the present position has been reached, both in terms of the debate about inclusion and the emergence of ECM, it is worth remembering some of the more recent landmarks that have led to the current situation, from the time of the 1970 Education Act.

Developments in ECM and SEN, 1970 – 2006

1970 — **Education Act.** All children brought within the education service, including those with an intelligence quotient (or IQ) deemed to be below 50, rather than being the responsibility of the health service.

1978 — *Report of the Committee of Enquiry into the Education of Handicapped Children and Young People* (often referred to as the Warnock Report). Chaired by Mary Warnock, it introduces the term 'Special Educational Needs' to encompass a further 18 per cent of the school population in addition to the 2 per cent catered for in special schools.

1981 — **Education Act** enshrines in law the statementing procedures to protect those with the greatest level of need within the SEN continuum.

1994 — *Code of Practice on the Identification and Assessment of Special Educational Needs* (first version) is published to address the needs of all the 20 per cent and not just the 2 per cent with a statement. A 5-stage approach to addressing those needs is advocated.

2001 —
i) *Code of Practice on the Identification and Assessment of Special Educational Needs* (revised) reduces the 5 stages of the original code in order to cut back on bureaucracy.

ii) **Special Educational Needs and Disability Act (SENDA)** strengthens the rights of parents to have a place in mainstream schools for their children. The Act places new duties on schools not to discriminate against pupils with disabilities and to make reasonable adjustments in order to include them.

NB: The SENDA, the SEN Regulations and the Code of Practice (revised) are sometimes referred to as the 'SEN Framework.'

2003 —
i) *Every Child Matters (ECM)* published as a result of Lord Laming's Inquiry into the death of Victoria Climbié.

ii) *The Report of the Special Schools Working Group* begins the shift back to recognising a continuing role for special schools, after the denigration of special schools in the 1980s and 1990s.

2004 —
i) **The Children Act** is passed and becomes the legislative framework for ECM.

ii) *Every Child Matters: Next Steps* sets out a timetable from 2004–08 to implement The Children Act.

iii) *Every Child Matters: Change for Children in Schools* is issued as a suite of documents specific to the role of schools, social care, the Criminal Justice System and health services.

iv) **The government's SEN strategy,** *Removing Barriers to Achievement* is published and incorporates some of the findings of *The Report of the Special Schools Working Group.*

2005 — *Special Educational Needs: A New Look* is published by Mary Warnock, who is concerned that, in the name of inclusion, too many pupils with SEN are being placed in mainstream schools.

2006 —
i) *House of Commons Education and Skills Committee's Report on Special Educational Needs* is published in 3 volumes, July 2006.

ii) *Conservative Party's Commission on Special Needs* is launched under the chairmanship of Sir Robert Balchin.

iii) *Government Response to the House of Commons Education and Skills Committee's Report on Special Educational Needs* published October 2006.

Making 'inclusion' include all provision

In tracking the evolution of the meaning of inclusion, it is worth remembering how there was a shift from the use of the term 'integration' in the 1980s, to using the term 'inclusion' in the 1990s.

Integration and inclusion

Integration was about integrating individuals into mainstream schools, with the onus being partly on the pupil with SEN to adapt to a mainstream environment.

Inclusion was used to signal a change as to how schools themselves could adapt to meet the needs of all the pupils who come to them.

The 1990s was a time when there was increasing awareness of the need to provide lifts and ramps to help wheelchair users and others with mobility problems to access buildings, and this included schools. Those with sensory impairments, the deaf and the sight impaired, bene-fited from technological advances that made it possible for some to access a mainstream curriculum for the first time. But a very sensible and realistic move to include more pupils in mainstream schools became for some enthusiasts of mainstream provision, proof that all could be included in mainstream education. This position overlooks the very real differences between those who need physical or technological adaptations to access the curriculum, and those with other kinds of needs, such as cognitive impairment, where no such adaptations are available. Warnock, in her introduction to Farrell's book, *Celebrating the Special School* says:

> *What has been wrong with the policy of inclusion has been the idea that if some children with special needs can flourish in the mainstream they all can. (Farrell, 2006: v)*

Although the new century has seen the growth of a common understanding about the need to maintain a range of provision, there is still a minority who would argue that, where inclusion appears not to be working, the fault lies entirely with schools who have failed to adapt sufficiently to meet all needs. In fact, most mainstream schools have worked extremely hard to include a wider range of pupils and have done so with a considerable degree of success. However, seeing it just in terms of what schools are achieving is only looking at one side of the issue. For it is not just a matter of how far *schools* have been successful in welcoming pupils with more complex needs, but whether the *pupils themselves* are comfortable in a mainstream envi-ronment. The idea that the greater the child's difficulties, the more it may be necessary to adapt the environment to suit their needs, is one that will be explored throughout this book.

A further aspect of the inclusion debate has been raised by those who have treated inclu-sion in mainstream schools as a human rights issue. This goes further than saying that there should be a right to choose a mainstream education. Instead, it puts forward the view that all schools must be prepared to accept all children and, as special schools stand in the way of this happening, special schools should close. As well as assuming that all pupils could have their needs addressed in a mainstream environment, including specialist teaching and equipment, and the therapies and medical support some of them depend upon, this viewpoint deprives parents of choice. It used to be the case that parents of children with SEN, had to fight for a mainstream place. Today, the situation has changed and parents are just as likely to be fighting for a place for their child in specialist provision. As Warnock says about inclusion in her latest publication, *Special Educational Needs: A New Look*:

> Let it be redefined so that it allows children to pursue the common goals of education in the environment within which they can best be taught and learn. (Warnock, 2005: 54)

If this is a matter of human rights, then surely it should be about the right of every child to receive an education appropriate to his or her needs.

In its SEN Strategy, *Removing Barriers to Achievement*, published in February 2004, the government tried to move the debate on by clarifying that inclusion does not mean including *all* pupils in mainstream schools, but including *all schools*, and, indeed, all types of specialist provision, within an inclusive education service. Although this was clearly spelt out in the document, it did not receive enough publicity to make it generally recognised or accepted as the way forward. Farrell suggests overcoming the problem of different interpretations by using a new expression:

> An alternative to inclusion, 'optimal education', involves mainstream and special schools working together in a joint enterprise of optimising the attainment, achievement, progress and personal development of pupils with SEN. (Farrell, 2006: 23)

He goes on to suggest that a key difference between inclusion and optimal education would be that 'there would be no presumption that special schools are revolving doors . . . for pupils with SEN whose real place is in the classroom' (Farrell, 2006: 24).

Farrell's idea of replacing 'inclusion' or 'an inclusive education service' with 'optimal education', would be one way forward. As he says himself, the ideas behind them are very similar. Both see a joined-up service, with mainstream and special schools working closely together to support pupils with SEN. The difference would be that Farrell sees 'optimal education' as meaning some children might be placed in specialist provision for most, if not all of their school career, whereas the 'revolving door' idea implies that pupils would be more likely to spend only *some* of their time in special education. Recently, the government itself has come up with a new expression. In its evidence to the House of Commons Education and Skills Committee, as part of the Inquiry into Special Educational Needs, (Autumn 2005–Spring 2006), the DfES clarified that the current view of government was to use the term a 'flexible continuum of provision', as an alternative to 'an inclusive education service'. It may be seen as an advantage in terms of getting away from arguments about inclusion and its meaning, that both 'optimal education' and 'a flexible continuum of provision' manage to avoid the word *inclusion* altogether. But whatever term is used, the idea is still the same, of seeing all schools as part of the same system, taking shared responsibility for meeting needs between them. This is a considerable advance on talking about special schools as 'segregated provision', and seeing mainstream and special schools as belonging to two discrete sectors. Both have so much to offer each other, and in encouraging local authorities to maintain a flexible continuum of provision, it should be easier for pupils – and staff – to move in and out of different settings. Pupils' needs are not static: they change over time, and a more flexible service should be able to respond by putting in place greater opportunities for children and young people to have different types of placements as their needs alter, including, short-term, part-time and dual-role placements.

Three types of placement

Short-term provision

Pupils may benefit from being in a more specialist setting for a short period of time and then be ready to return to mainstream classes after a period of intensive help. At present, the statementing process makes it harder to put this fully in place.

Part-time placements

Some pupils have sessions when they go to a different school. Children may be in special schools part-time, when they are undergoing assessment, using it as a step towards reintegration, or to give pupils who are likely to stay in special schools, some experience of a wider peer group. Likewise, pupils in mainstream schools may have some sessions in a special school.

Dual placements

These can also work both ways. Pupils may have dual registration, dividing their time between two settings, for instance, taking part in lessons at a mainstream school, while continuing to be on the roll of a special school, or vice versa. Over time, pupils are likely to reach a stage where it is clear which environment will suit them best.

Putting in place more flexible arrangements for meeting pupils' needs, ties in very neatly with the government's Every Child Matters agenda, which places children and families at the centre and builds round them the services they need.

Making every child matter

The Green Paper, *Every Child Matters*, and the Children Act 2004 that enshrined it in law, looks at how to meet the needs of children and families in a more holistic way. This involves the main services used by families – education, health and social care, in particular – working much more closely together and being more readily accessible. To help bring this about, the former Local Education Authorities (LEAs) are disappearing and becoming part of Children's Services, with a Director of Children's Services, rather than a Director of Education.

The Children Act

Under the Act, Local Authorities are required to:

- Appoint a Director of Children's Services

- Appoint a Lead Member for Children's Services

- Promote the educational achievement of children in care

By 2008, they must establish children's trusts to deliver frontline services, working with local partners from the public, private, community and voluntary sectors in offering support to children and families.

At school level as well, there is an expectation of more joined-up working. Children's centres are at the forefront of this new approach for pre-school children and some are being based with primary schools. All schools are expected to contribute to the Extended Schools programme, offering childcare, as well as a range of activities between the hours of 8 a.m. and 6 p.m. to children, their families and the local community. In other words, schools are taking on a role that sees them being at the centre of their communities, rather than being there solely for the benefit of their own pupils.

Children's Centres and Extended Schools

Children's Centres

- Early years provision for 0–5 year olds, with a qualified teacher in charge

- Support for parents

- Access to health and social care

- Referral pathways to other specialist services

Extended Schools

- All schools to be involved by 2010, working collaboratively to provide services between them

- All primary-aged pupils able to access childcare all year from 8 a.m. to 6 p.m.

- All secondary schools open all year round from 8 a.m. to 6 p.m.

- Varied menu of activities, such as study support, homework clubs, breakfast clubs, catch-up classes, opportunities for the gifted and talented, dance, drama, music, sport and ICT

- Support for parents and family learning

- Health advice and referral pathways to other specialist services

- Community to have access to facilities and lifelong learning opportunities

As Extended Provision becomes the norm, ways will need to be found of ensuring that pupils with special educational needs and disabilities are not excluded from the opportunities offered to their peers. Transport and additional staffing will need to be considered. For children attending special schools, there will be the question of whether they access after-school clubs in or near their school, or in their home locality, which may be some distance away.

Fundamental to Every Child Matters are the five outcomes, which were decided in discussion with children and young people, who said they were the ones that mattered most to them. While the joining up of services will take longer to achieve, and has not yet impinged significantly on the work of all schools, the five outcomes are already beginning to pervade all aspects of school life.

The 5 outcomes of ECM

1 Being healthy

2 Staying safe

3 Enjoying and achieving

4 Making a positive contribution

5 Achieving economic well-being

Work in progress

While it will take time to change structures and practices, to break down the divisions between professionals and create more productive joint working processes between services, there is at least clarity about what needs to be done and how to set about creating a better future for children, young people and their families. Although considerable progress has also been made in agreeing what needs to be put in place to improve provision for pupils with SEN, there are still areas of uncertainty. As a result of its Inquiry into SEN during 2005–06, the House of Commons Education and Skills Committee, while in agreement with the need for the full range of provision, itemised some of the difficulties and called upon the government to take a fresh look at SEN, in order to:

- Develop a national framework, giving minimum standards for the range of provision that should exist in every area

- Undertake a radical review of statementing (which was also called for by the Audit Commission in 2002, when they discovered that 68% of the funding available for SEN was being spent on the 3% with statements)

- Resolve the contradiction in what has been said about whether special schools are likely to 'shrink'(as suggested in the SEN Strategy), or whether the present numbers in special schools (roughly 1.4% of the school population) are to remain static (as suggested by the DfES in its evidence to the Select Committee)

- Ensure that *inclusion*, in the sense of including all pupils in the setting or settings that best meets their needs, is more widely understood

In its reply, the government rejected the idea that a fresh look at SEN was necessary, because it felt that sufficient progress was being made. It agreed that a national framework is desirable, but saw this coming about as a result of ECM and the implementation of the five outcomes, integrated planning and multi-agency working. Its view on statementing was that there are some improvements, with a lessening of the differences between authorities in the numbers who gain statements and a general move to get money into schools without recourse to the statementing process. The government did agree, however, that the Chief Inspector for Schools (HMCI), should carry out a review of progress in 2009/10:

> We have asked Her Majesty's Chief Inspector of Schools to consider progress in 2009/2010. We will consider, in the light of HMCI's advice, whether the present framework for SEN, or particular features of it, should be reviewed and what further action should be taken to achieve better outcomes for children with SEN and/or disabilities and their families. (Section 1, paragraph 17)

Meanwhile, the Interim Recommendations of the Conservative Commission on Special Needs are fully supportive of the need to maintain a range of provision. Indeed, the suggestion is made that there might need to be more special schools. This raises an interesting point for discussion. If more pupils are being identified with conditions such as attention deficit/hyperactivity disorder (AD/HD), autistic spectrum disorders (ASD), behaviour, emotional and social difficulties (BESD), as well as mental health problems, it could be argued that a greater range of specialist provision is needed. This need not necessarily mean more special schools, although it could include that option as part of the solution.

A 'flexible continuum of provision' in practice

At the heart of this book are four chapters which give examples of the many and varied ways that a flexible range of provision is beginning to emerge. The first of these (Chapter 2) looks at developments from the perspective of mainstream schools, which is where the vast majority of pupils with special educational needs have always been educated. Case studies are included of schools from across the age range, from a children's centre to an academy, and from a first school with a very high percentage of special needs, to a secondary school for girls, where numbers with SEN used to be well below average, but are now increasing substantially. The next two chapters (3 and 4) switch to the perspective of the special school, although the mainstream element is very much present in the examples of federations, partnerships and co-located schools.

Chapter 3 looks at a variety of day provision, while Chapter 4 concentrates on schools offering residential placements. To give a broader picture, case studies are included of schools in Northern Ireland and Wales. Chapter 5 turns to the development of outreach, advisory and support services, as well as pupil referral units (PRUs), all of which are available to support schools in including children and young people who have special educational needs.

It has been possible to include only a few examples of some of the innovative and exciting ways in which schools and services are exploring how best to include fully all pupils, and make the five outcomes a reality for them. It is hoped that this glimpse will be enough to bring readers in touch with some of the extraordinarily imaginative and inspiring ways that a flexible continuum of provision is being created.

As Tutt and Barthorpe state:

> Every child must matter and every child must feel equally valued. All pupils and students deserve an education tailored to their individual aptitudes and interests, but for those who have special educational needs, the personalisation of their schooling requires that much more thought and attention, so that they can maximise their potential within a flexible and inclusive education service. (2006:12)

Final thoughts

- Has your concept of inclusion changed at all since reading this chapter, and if so, in what way has it altered?

- Do you agree with the concept of a flexible continuum of provision? If not, what would you put in its place? If you do agree, list the types of provision you would include as part of the continuum.

- Do you think it is possible or useful to identify pupils who are disabled but do not have SEN, or who have SEN but are not disabled?

- Do you know of any children who you think could be described as one but not the other? What is the nature of their SEN or disability?

- What do you think are the dangers in labelling children? Could we do without labels altogether?

 ## Recommended Reading

Department for Education and Skills (2004) *Removing Barriers to Achievement: The Government's SEN Strategy*. Nottingham: DfES.

Green Paper (2003) *Every Child Matters*. London: The Stationery Office.

Tutt, R. and Barthorpe, T. (2006) *All Inclusive? Moving Beyond the SEN Inclusion Debate*. Devon: The Iris Press.

Warnock, M. (2005) *Special Educational Needs: A New Look*. No.11 in a series of policy discussions. UK: Philosophy of Education Society.

CHAPTER 2

Mainstream provision for special educational needs

This chapter is concerned with the majority of children with special educational needs who are catered for in mainstream provision. As well as discussing different types of support, in terms of the curriculum, facilities and staffing, four examples are given of very different settings from across the age range:

■ A children's centre

■ A first school, which is about to become a primary school, and which has a very high percentage of pupils with SEN

■ A secondary school for girls, with a mixed sixth form, which has had a below average number of students with SEN

■ An academy, with resourced provision for students who have:

i)   behavioural, emotional and social difficulties (BESD)
ii) physical disabilities (PD)

The mainstream perspective

Until recently, much of the debate about the meaning of inclusion has centred round whether or not a small proportion of pupils with SEN should be educated in special schools, or whether mainstream schools should be able to include all pupils, including those with the most complex needs. In fact, it could be seen as odd that so much time has been spent debating this matter, when the vast majority of pupils with SEN have always been in mainstream schools anyway. In the last few years, most of these schools have made enormous strides in adapting both the environment and the curriculum to be more readily accessible to pupils with a wide range of needs.

As mentioned in the previous chapter, before the 1978 report chaired by Mary Warnock, pupils in mainstream schools who had difficulty in learning for all or part of their school careers, had not been identified as a group who needed to be given particular attention. The Warnock committee changed that by using the term 'special educational needs' to cover a further 18 per cent of the school population, in addition to the 2 per cent who were being educated in special schools. As the 1981 Education Act that followed largely ignored this group, to concentrate on devising the statementing procedures for those with the most complex needs, it was not until the first version of the Code of Practice for SEN in 1994, (revised 2001), that much notice was taken of trying to meet the needs of the much wider group of pupils who had always been in mainstream schools, but whose needs had not been systematically addressed.

Now that the debate has moved on to focus on creating a flexible continuum of provision within which schools and services work closely together, it is important to start at the mainstream end of the SEN continuum because this is where most of the pupils with SEN have always been educated. Mainstream schools have made substantial adjustments in order to meet a more diverse range of needs, with some developing resourced provision.

Resourced provision

Resourced provision in mainstream schools, both primary and secondary, can take many forms, including:

- Designated schools being adapted to take, for instance, pupils who have physical disabilities

- Bases or units where pupils with SEN may go for part of the school day, either to receive specialist teaching, or to be supported in other ways (learning support units, or LSUs, are an example of unit provision and are described later in this chapter)

- Special classes in which pupils with SEN are placed, where smaller numbers enable them to receive additional attention

Some special schools also have bases or units to enable them to give support to pupils with particular needs.

There are many reasons why mainstream schools are having to make considerable adjustments:

1 To support the growing number of children who have been adversely affected by the lack of a stable, nurturing home environment and who arrive at school without the pre-requisite skills for learning in a school situation

2 To cater for the increase in children diagnosed as having a range of conditions, such as attention deficit/hyperactivity disorder (AD/HD), autistic spectrum disorders (ASD), dyspraxia, and dyscalculia

3 To find ways of helping those who develop mental health problems, become disaffected, or who exhibit very challenging behaviour

4 To accommodate pupils who would previously have attended special schools and who are now in their local schools, such as those with moderate learning difficulties (MLD)

5 To adapt the way the school works in order to put in place the Every Child Matters agenda

Some of these points will be referred to in discussing the examples of different types of provision given in this chapter. The case studies have been chosen to illustrate how four very different institutions have sought ways of including pupils with special educational needs, as well as any changes they have made in the light of Every Child Matters. The first one is a children's centre, which is included because the development of these centres is a key part of addressing Every Child Matters, and such centres are instrumental in helping to identify and address any learning difficulties children may have before they reach statutory school age. This is followed by an example of a first school, which has a very high percentage of special needs and has developed an unusual approach to curriculum delivery, in order to include all children. The third case study is of a girls' secondary school with a mixed sixth form, where a more individualised approach was taken to meet the needs of a small percentage of pupils with SEN, but which has adapted successfully to accommodate a far wider range of students. The final example is an academy, which is resourced to cater for those with physical disabilities and those who have behavioural, emotional and social difficulties (BESD), and which has found a number of ways of including a very diverse population. The examples in this chapter, therefore, cover the first elements of a flexible range of provision:

A continuum of SEN provision

Children's centres

+

Mainstream schools	Resourced mainstream schools	Special schools (day)	Special schools (residential)

← pupil referral units (PRUs), advisory, support and outreach services →

Some children's centres are attached to schools, while others are separate entities. PRUs and the various services support all types and phases of schools between them.

Questions for reflection

■ Do you think it is true that pre-school settings and schools for younger pupils are having to adapt what they do for children whose ability to listen, speak and share is more limited than used to be the case?

■ Do you think it is the case that schools are having to adjust to a broader range of needs? If so, are there other reasons for this changed population, besides the ones listed previously?

■ Whether or not you feel there has been a noticeable change, do you think that the thrust of ECM will help to address these types of issues?

Childcare and education for the pre-school child

The lack of readiness for school in some young children has already been mentioned and there have been concerns expressed, particularly among those who teach the youngest pupils, that more are arriving in reception classes without the language and social skills they need to be ready for school. In an article in 2003, David Bell, the Chief Inspector at the time, talked of children receiving a 'disrupted and dishevelled upbringing', and, as a result, their verbal and behavioural skills being at an all-time low:

> It is difficult to get hard statistical evidence on what is happening across the country, but if you talk to a lot of primary head teachers, they will say that youngsters appear less well prepared for school than they have ever been before. (Daily Telegraph, 31 August 2003, Julie Henry)

Sue Palmer, in her book *Toxic Childhood*, suggests that the three key principles children need to learn in order to change from 'tantrum-throwing two-year-olds to relatively civilised pre-teens' are:

1 The ability to maintain attention, including on items that are not of great importance to them

2 An understanding of *deferred gratification*, so that they accept rewards are not always immediate

3 The reality of living in a group means that their own needs have to be balanced against the needs of others

One of the ways in which the government is trying to ensure that young children start formal schooling able to stay on task, to accept direction and to work happily in a group, is through the creation of children's centres, starting by placing them in the most deprived areas of the country. In addition to the general aim of working with parents and children to promote the all-round development of pre-schoolers, the centres have a particular role to play in identifying children with SEN and providing early intervention and support.

One of the oldest examples is the Thomas Coram Children's Centre in London, which has existed under different names since the 18th century. In 1998, it became an Early Excellence Centre, and in 2003 it became one of the first children's centres. Providing for children and families in this way has been made possible by the voluntary and state sectors working together, with the Coram Family Charity providing the land and the local authority paying the costs. This is a good example of the government's drive, as part of ECM, to see the state and voluntary sectors working more closely together, pooling their resources in order to provide more effectively for children and their families.

Case study: The Thomas Coram Centre for Children and Families

The three-acre site, which houses the children's centre, a parents' centre and a wide range of other support services and activities, seems like an oasis in a built-up area. It is owned by the Coram Family Charity and the Centre is funded by the Borough of Camden.

The children's centre caters for the equivalent of 106 full-time places divided as follows:

- 12 places for babies aged 6 months to 2 years

- 24 places for toddlers aged 2–3 years

- 70 places in the nursery for 3–5 year olds

The integrated day care and early education is available for 48 weeks a year from 8 a.m. to 6 p.m. Children up to the age of 11 join in after-school clubs and holiday playschemes. In conjunction with the Coram parents' centre, about 600 children, parents and carers use the facilities each week. They speak over 50 different community languages. Parents and carers can attend a wide variety of courses and are helped to do so by the onsite crèche facility.

Up to 30 per cent of the children have SEN: 20 per cent are admitted as referrals and are given priority and a further 10 per cent or so will be identified after they have been admitted. The head teacher of the children's centre, Bernadette Duffy, says that she can meet the needs of all the children provided they have enough additional support. Children with identified SEN are integrated as fully as possible, sometimes with one-to-one support. A few children have needed two-to-one staffing. These include some children with autistic spectrum disorders who, Bernadette Duffy has found, can be the hardest to integrate. She says:

Before a child comes to us, we have a multidisciplinary meeting, which includes the parents, to look at what the child and the family needs so that it can be put in place before he or she starts.

Music therapy, speech and language therapy, and physiotherapy, are available at the Centre. Health and social care, as well as a child psychology service, are among the many services that share the same campus.

To ensure that the quality of the provision remains high throughout the extended hours and days the children's centre is open, the head, deputy head and assistant head work closely together as a team, with a timetable flexible enough to ensure that at least one of them is always available and on site.

The Centre has close links with local schools to which children transfer, including a special school, so that as much care can be taken over transition when pupils leave, as it is when they first arrive.

Teaching in a children's centre requires the ability to move outside traditional working patterns, both in terms of the range of professionals who will be close colleagues, and in the sense of breaking away from the usual pattern of terms and holiday periods. Contact with families is likely to be greater, which is particularly important in terms of the kinds of families the centres may be supporting. At the Thomas Coram Centre, for instance, there are refugee families, asylum seekers, the homeless and the unemployed. Having a safe and stimulating environment, indoors and out, provides the children of these families with vital opportunities to play and explore their environment. It gives their families much needed support and the chance of acquiring new skills to help them as parents and to increase their chances of future employment.

Successful strategies

- Differentiating the size of the groups so that the youngest children have the highest level of individual care

- Understanding the child's needs in the context of the family

- Having support organised and in place before a child with SEN is admitted

- Linking with receiving schools to ease the transition to full-time schooling

- Having a leadership team that works flexibly, instead of sticking to a more traditional, term-time only timetable

---

Points to ponder

- What do you think are the advantages of integrated childcare and education for the very young?

- What do you consider to be the disadvantages?

- Do you think there are other ways of supporting children and families, particularly in areas of deprivation?

Young pupils of school age

At the time of Warnock's report, 2 per cent of pupils were being educated in special schools. Today, the figure is nearer 1.2 per cent. This is not a huge change, but it does mean that some pupils who previously would have attended a special school are now in their local schools. The statementing procedures were brought in to cover the 2 per cent in special schools. Today, statements have risen from 2 per cent to 2.9 per cent, with well over half the pupils who have statements being educated in mainstream schools. With the SEN Codes of Practice (1994, revised 2001), there has been an emphasis on the importance of the role of a special educational needs coordinator (SENCO), to bring together the support all pupils with SEN may need, and to decide how it will be delivered.

In the late 1980s, there was a movement away from taking pupils out of the classroom to give them individual support and an emphasis instead on delivering that extra help, (often in the form of a teaching assistant and sometimes in the form of a teacher), inside the classroom. There were advantages and disadvantages with both methods.

In-class support	Withdrawal
Advantages	**Advantages**
Child feels included	Child enjoys individual attention
Extra help is available to more pupils	Child can be taught specific skills
Disadvantages	**Disadvantages**
Child may feel more self-conscious	Child misses out on class activities
Help may be less individually targeted	Skills taught may not transfer to the classroom situation

Figure 2.1 Methods of support

Pupils themselves expressed a range of views. Some felt more self-conscious and conspicuous with a teaching assistant supporting them in class; others did not like to be seen as the ones who were being taken out. Some preferred to stay working with their friends, while others liked the individual attention of working on their own with a member of staff. Once the prevailing view had gone from withdrawing pupils as a matter of course to giving support in the classroom, a more reasonable approach crept in, which was based on the child's needs and how they could best be addressed. For some time now, there has been a much more flexible approach, where the needs and feelings of the child are seen as paramount and this guides the decisions about the kind of help pupils should receive and where it will be delivered. This approach was apparent in the first case study, where, in the more informal setting of a pre-school environment, children were able to engage in activities alongside their peers for most of the time, but there were still occasions when a child might be overwhelmed and taken to a quieter area, or more hyperactive children might have additional times for letting off steam, away from a group activity.

As children become older, the demands on them increase and a flexible approach to meeting their needs becomes even more important. The next three case studies illustrate some ways in which this flexibility around the needs of the child is being addressed, rather than seeing inclusion in terms of keeping the child in the classroom at all costs. This flexibility has moved beyond discussions simply about where support should be given, to looking at different ways in which it can be delivered. The concerns that some children are arriving at school not ready to learn have already been raised and children's centres have been mentioned as a way of helping to support very young children's all-round development. As most children will not have had the benefit of a children's centre, schools have looked at ways they might prepare children for formal schooling and make up for some of the early learning experiences they have missed. One answer has been the creation of nurture classes or nurture groups.

Nurture groups and the Boxall Profile

The Boxall Profile is named after Marjorie Boxall, who was an educational psychologist. In 1969, she started nurture groups for children whose home circumstances meant that they arrived at school not ready for formal education. In order to assess the stage of development each one had reached, she created the Boxall Profile. This consists of two checklists. The first one is a developmental strand, that assesses the child's early learning experiences. The second strand is a diagnostic one that measures the child's emotional development and where any difficulties may lie.

The school in the second case study assesses all its pupils using the Boxall Profile and the children that staff feel could benefit will join a nurture group. The head teacher, Sue Eagle, makes the valid point that 'Nurture groups only work in a nurturing school'. As almost half her pupils have special educational needs, and many come from disadvantaged backgrounds, the head teacher has been able to gear the whole school to having this nurturing environment for all its pupils. The approach to the curriculum is to have less emphasis on following a set pattern for teaching literacy and numeracy, and more on engaging pupils in their own learning in a number of different ways, including Philosophy for Children and contextual drama (Mantle of the Expert).

Mantle of the Expert

This is a way of creating realistic learning contexts through drama, although the work involved goes beyond acting to incorporate almost any area of the curriculum. Devised by Dorothy Heathcote, a renowned educator, a fictional world is created in which every child has a role as an expert. For instance, in a topic such as 'Running a Bear Sanctuary', one child might be a vet, one a keeper, and another an accountant. The children become 'expert' in their roles and work together to contribute their expertise to run a successful venture.

Philosophy for Children (based on Socratic dialogue)

This approach encourages children, from the youngest pupils upwards, to learn to ask questions and to have enquiring minds. They engage with the curriculum and become involved in their own learning by being able to distinguish between questions and statements. They learn to discuss and debate, to give reasons for why they agree or disagree with someone and to justify their ideas.

The school's inclusion policy is laid out as a flow chart. A simplified version (without all the subheadings) is given in Figure 2.2. This can be photocopied and used as a point of comparison with schools' existing policies, or as a starting point when such policies are being discussed.

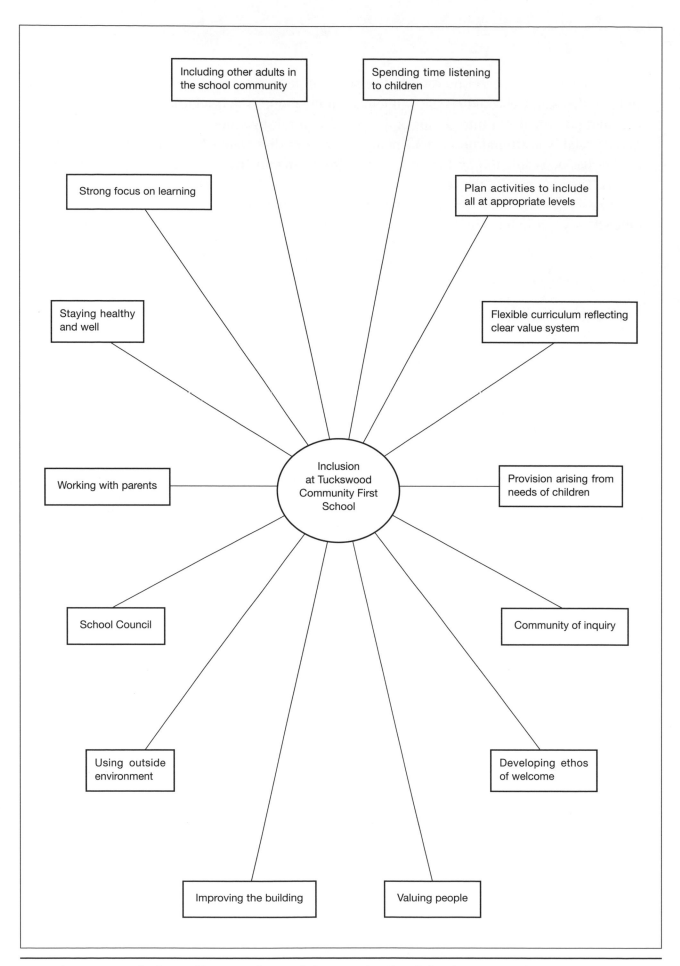

Figure 2.2 Inclusion policy at Tuckswood Community First School
Every Child Included, Paul Chapman Publishing © Rona Tutt, 2007

Case study: Tuckswood Community First School, Norfolk

The school has 110 pupils aged 4–8 years. It will shortly extend its age range to become a primary school. Over 40 per cent of the children have SEN, and the school is in a poor socio-economic area. However, it is well supported by the community, as it has always been seen as a hub of local activity. A pre-school playgroup shares the school's premises, but is under separate management.

The head teacher, Sue Eagle, tries to meet the needs of any pupils whose parents want them to be admitted. Children's needs are always seen as central, so although children are learning alongside their peers for most of the time, they will be supported in class, taken individually or in small groups, as appropriate. Sue Eagle says:

If you get the curriculum right, then it is possible to include almost all children. You set out your whole school beliefs and values, and then decide how the curriculum will be delivered.

As well as Mantle of the Expert and Philosophy for Children, the approaches previously identified, pupils follow the 'Massage in Schools' programme, where they learn to do simple massage techniques on each other. As well as the Nurture Room, there is a Light Sensory Room that all children can enjoy, and to which some of those who have sufficient insight into their own difficulties are allowed to take themselves when they need time to reflect and calm down. In addition, the following are available to those who need them:

■ Social skills groups, where pupils learn to interact and communicate more effectively

■ Individual counselling on site for one day a week, where pupils can be put forward for sessions on the recommendation of a teacher or a parent

■ Anger management courses run by outside professionals

■ Solution Focused Therapy (sometimes known as Brief Therapy, because it aims to achieve results quickly by seeking solutions for the future rather than solving problems from the past) is delivered in conjunction with the local authority's Behaviour and Education Support Team (BEST).

The school has links with a nearby special school and a pupil from there may have some sessions at Tuckwood, or a pupil from Tuckswood may spend time in the special school. The school has also taken part in 'managed moves' of pupils who have been excluded from other schools. Sue Eagle is very clear that when this happens, the necessary support must be provided to minimise the risk of the child 'failing' again. The school's anti-bullying policy, which is contained within a *Policy for Ensuring Positive and Happy Relationships*, uses the principles of 'restorative justice.' This brings together the bully and the bullied within a set framework that tries to resolve conflicts and re-establish good relationships. Every class has its own council, which feeds in to the School Council. Decisions go back to the classes to be ratified.

After-school clubs run until 4.30 p.m. These include football, mini-squash, dance, drama, French and Spanish. Family learning is encouraged. There is a Parents Support Group that meets during the day and parents come in every morning for early activities. Some also support their children in the classroom. Workshops are put on for parents to gain a fuller understanding of the curriculum. They are seen to be full partners in the education of their children.

A copy of Tuckswood's School Improvement and Development Plan is set out as a photo-copiable resource on page 20. Although there is further documentation to back up the various elements of the plan, having it presented as a mind map on one side of A4 helps to give an overview of what the plan is trying to achieve. As it is based on ECM, some schools who have not aligned their plans with the five outcomes, may find it particularly useful as a starting point for discussion next time their own plan is being updated. Others may like to use it as an example of how to encapsulate the essence of their own school improvement and/or development plans on a single sheet.

Successful strategies

- Being prepared to try out new approaches that may support all pupils, including those with SEN

- Being prepared to provide flexibly for pupils with SEN, taking into consideration their needs and their views

- Having a range of techniques and approaches to support pupils with BESD, including accepting 'managed moves' with the support such pupils need fully in place before admission

- Using 'restorative justice' as a means of resolving conflict between the bullied and the bullying

- Engaging parents by encouraging them to participate in the first or last part of the school day, and involving the wider community in the life of the school so that it is seen as a centre of community activity

---

Points to ponder

- Does your own school use any innovative approaches for pupils with SEN? If so, which have been most successful and how do you know?

- Whether or not you are used to trying out new ideas, what else do you think you might try as a way of helping pupils who have SEN, including those with behavioural difficulties?

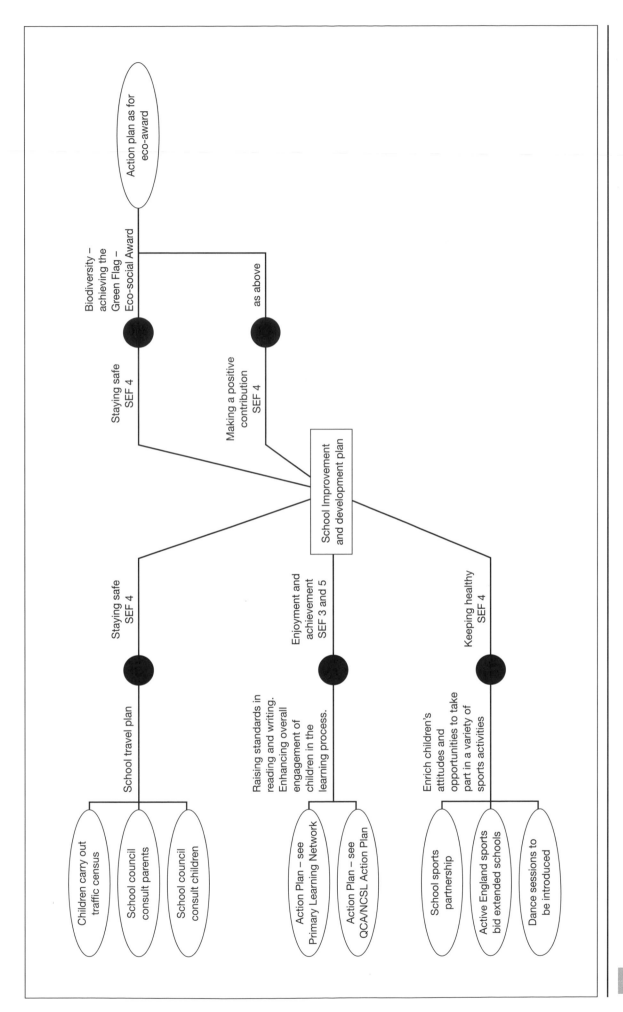

Figure 2.3 School improvement and development plan for Tuckswood Community First School
Every Child Included, Paul Chapman Publishing © Rona Tutt, 2007

The secondary phase of education

The secondary phase of education, in particular, has seen the appearance of a wide variety of schools. Most mainstream secondary schools are now specialist schools with specialisms in one or more areas of the curriculum. More recently, a growing number of academies have become established. Grammar schools and a few city technology colleges continue to be part of the existing provision, while trust schools are on the horizon. As mentioned earlier on in the chapter, some of these schools will be resourced schools, which are equipped in a variety of ways to provide for pupils with SEN. An example of a resourced secondary school is given in the final case study in this chapter.

Although primary schools will be able to draw on the services of educational psychologists and many other professionals, a particularly wide and growing range of personnel are now working in secondary schools, many of them connected to students with SEN. Indeed, it has reached the stage where some students have been heard to remark that they do not want any more people involved in their lives. Others, of course, may be anxious to receive more support. These are just some examples of personnel who have arrived in schools more recently:

- **Connexions personal advisers** who provide advice and guidance to pupils aged 13–19, and will continue to support young people up to the age of 25 who have SEN. They have a particular role to play in advising students on training and career opportunities.

- **Learning mentors** are salaried staff who work with school and college students and bridge the academic and pastoral support roles, helping students to overcome any barriers to learning and achievement. Originally employed as part of the Excellence in Cities initiative, which brought extra resources to the most deprived areas of the country, they are now established in many schools, helping students by taking a personal interest in their progress and well-being.

- **Counsellors** are becoming increasingly common, as schools seek to provide for those from troubled home backgrounds, those who exhibit disruptive or challenging behaviour, or those with emotional problems, such as eating disorders.

So one of the ways that schools have changed, partly in line with the changing complexity of the school population, is the growing number of different people and agencies that schools are able to call upon. This means that special educational needs coordinators (SENCOs), particularly in large secondary schools, need to keep careful records of the support students are receiving. The secondary school in the third case study, Tolworth Girls' School, only had about 8 per cent of its students with identified SEN a few years ago, although it had always had an inclusive outlook. Today, the figure has nearly doubled and the SENCO, Tricia Benson, has undertaken 'provision mapping' as a way of keeping track of what extra support pupils are allocated.

Provision mapping

Provision mapping has many uses. It is a way of charting, or mapping, what provision is available and how it is being used.

In terms of SEN, it has been used:

■ To document the range of support available and who is receiving it

■ As a tool to manage delegated SEN funding, by showing the costs of staffing and other resources and detailing how the money allocated is being spent

---

Figure 2.4 is an example of the format used at Tolworth to map the provision available to students with SEN in the sixth form. The following terms may need a note of explanation:

■ **ASDAN** awards are used by schools and colleges to motivate, in particular, lower achieving pupils. They offer a wide range of activity-based modules at accessible levels

■ **Option support groups** offer alternative programmes, including college courses, for students who need an alternative curriculum, rather than following the usual exam courses

■ Tolworth has used some of the money from being a *Leading Edge* school, to create a **Leading Edge programme** for some of the most challenging students. Through good behaviour, they can earn special trips and outings, as well as a more personalised curriculum geared to keeping them motivated and in education

Headings that do not appear in Figure 2.4, but are on the provision mapping chart for younger pupils are:

■ Breakfast club

■ Booster club

■ Reading 'catch up'

■ Withdrawal literacy group

■ Curriculum support group

■ Mentoring by trained teaching assistants

■ Speech and language therapy

■ Social communication group

■ Medicinal intervention

■ Homework club

Surname	First name	Form	Stage on the Code of Practice	Difficulty	TA support number of hours (in class)	TA support (one-to-one)	Counselling	CAMHS	Sensory impairment	Leading Edge	AS DAN	Off-site provision	Breakfast club	Educational Psychologist	Social Services	EBD mentoring	Nurse	EAL	Option support group

Figure 2.4 Tolworth Girls' School and Centre for Continuing Education: Provision mapping

Every Child Included, Paul Chapman Publishing © Rona Tutt, 2007

Schools or services wishing to undertake provision mapping will be able to adapt the format to their own circumstances. (NB Although students with English as an additional Language (EAL), are included on the same sheet, it is made clear whether or not they have SEN when the form is filled in.)

Case study: Tolworth Girls' School and Centre for Continuing Education

Tolworth is a community school for 1,050 girls aged 11–18, with a mixed sixth form of 360. It is a Leading Edge School, a Training School, and in September 2005 became a Specialist Technology School. A unit for students with autistic spectrum disorders (ASD) is likely to be added to the school's provision shortly.

Over the last four years, the school has gone from having only 8 per cent of pupils with SEN to nearly doubling that number. The school is non-selective and has always had a strong commitment to including any student who, with support, can benefit from a mainstream curriculum. The school is fully adapted to take students who are severely physically disabled and has coped with those who have very little ability to control their movements, including relying on communication aids instead of speaking.

The school has mixed ability classes apart from maths and science. Staff in the Learning Support Department work as a team, with teaching assistants working alongside teachers to support students in the classroom whenever possible. Although every effort will be made to keep students in class, when necessary, they can be removed to the Time Out area of the Learning Support Base. Teachers and support staff share responsibility for delivering the extra sessions available to pupils with SEN (as itemised previously).

Tricia Benson, the SENCO, gives a high priority to training for all her staff. There are visiting teachers for those with sensory impairments and the school links with local special schools for an exchange of students for some sessions when the need arises on either side.

With the growth in the number of pupils exhibiting behavioural difficulties, one teacher in the Learning Support Department takes the lead on behavioural issues. Both she and the SENCO have run emotional literacy classes and anger management courses for Years 9 and 10. Staff work closely with the school's educational psychologist, the heads of department and heads of year, so that the department itself is seen as an integral part of the school.

There is a qualified counsellor for three days a week and, as an extension to this work with individuals, Relate (formerly known as The Marriage Guidance Council), is starting work with whole families on relationships. Clarissa Williams, the head teacher, is concerned about students who have mental health problems. School refusers in year 11 may be placed in the local pupil referral unit (PRU) or funded for flexible learning programmes.

All classes are represented on a very active School Council. Students are encouraged to report any bullying they have witnessed by placing the details in a Bullying Box. Any incidents are followed up rigorously. As well as homework clubs and other school-related opportunities, there are enrichment activities, including some run with the support of the local Music and Arts Service. All students have the chance of working for the Duke of Edinburgh Awards Scheme.

There is no doubt that the school population at Tolworth has changed significantly in recent years. The school has responded positively by finding new ways of including students with severe physical disabilities and a range of other conditions. Clarissa Williams, the head teacher, has worked with her staff to identify any difficulties and to put in place programmes that will prevent vulnerable students from becoming disenchanted. She says:

There is often a link between the child's family situation and the growing trend of depression and emotional disruption, which is sometimes not addressed until it is too late. We make every effort to create a more appetising special programme of classes with short-term, achievable goals, so that disengaged students can experience what is it like to attain, gain work experience and take part in fun activities that offer an alternative to the academic route for those who need it.

Successful strategies

- Using provision mapping as a way of recording the support students receive, so that it can be monitored and evaluated in terms of the progress it has enabled students to make

- Having clear roles and responsibilities for the Learning Support Team and embedding its work in the life of the school

- Having a range of options to support pupils with weak literacy skills, differentiated for those who respond to a 'booster class' approach and those who need longer-term support

- Using a variety of approaches to support those whose behaviour acts as a barrier to learning, including a 'time out' facility, mentoring, counselling and the support of professionals beyond the school

- Keeping the disaffected in school, by rewarding good behaviour in ways that motivate them and by having a flexible, individualised approach to the curriculum, including how and where it will be delivered

---

Points to ponder

- What do you see as the advantages of provision mapping?

- Do you think it would, and could, be used in your school or service and if so in what way?

- Schools sometimes state that it is easier to accommodate pupils with severe physical disabilities rather than those with severe learning difficulties, or those who have behavioural problems. Do you agree, and if so what are your reasons?

Resourced provision

In a report entitled, *Inclusion: Does it Matter Where Pupils are Taught?* which Ofsted published in July 2006, the following conclusions were reached:

> *The most important factor in determining the best outcomes for pupils with learning difficulties and disabilities (LDD) is not the type but the quality of the provision. Effective provision was distributed equally in the mainstream and special schools visited, but there was more good and outstanding provision in resourced mainstream schools than elsewhere. Pupil referral units (PRUs) were the least successful of all settings visited. (Ofsted, 2006: 2)*

The report also points out that it is not so much the additional resources, including the contribution of teaching assistants, that results in good quality intervention and progress by pupils, but the following:

- The involvement of a specialist teacher

- Good assessment

- Work tailored to challenge pupils sufficiently

- Commitment from school leaders to ensure good progress for all pupils

In addition, the report suggests that it is pupils with BESD who received the least effective support and who are most likely to receive it too late.

One of the ways that schools, and particularly secondary schools, have addressed this issue has been by creating learning support units (LSUs), which are one type of resourced provision.

Learning support units (LSUs)

LSUs came into being in 1999, as part of the Excellence in Cities initiative, although some schools had similar provision before that date.

There are over 1,500 LSUs, but only about 120 in primary schools. They are school-based centres that are mainly designed for the disaffected and those at risk of exclusion. However, some schools use them, not just for improving behaviour, attendance and attitudes, but to provide extra support for others who can benefit from it.

Schools will call them by a variety of names depending on the focus of their work and the terminology the school prefers to employ. Whereas pupil referral units (PRUs), are offsite provision, LSUs are onsite provision, usually consisting of a room or suite of rooms that can accommodate a group of pupils for all or part of a day.

The final case study in this chapter is of an academy that has resourced provision for pupils who have behavioural, emotional and social difficulties (BESD), as well as additional provision for those with physical disabilities (PD).

Academies

City technology colleges (CTCs), introduced by the Conservatives, are seen as the forerunners to the academies programme. Academies are described as state-funded independent schools, because they operate independently of the local authority in which they are situated and have greater freedom to innovate.

The first Academies opened in 2003 and by 2006, there were over 30, with many more in the pipeline, suggesting that the government will reach its target of having 200 in place before long. They are situated in areas of disadvantage, where they replace one or more schools, or are built because there is a demand for additional places in that area.

Under the scheme, private sponsors from business, faith or voluntary groups, contribute up to £2 million and in exchange are allowed to appoint the majority of governors. Sponsors may be individuals or corporate bodies.

Academies were put in place to give fresh opportunities and new facilities to pupils who live in the most disadvantaged areas. As they are not bound by the same admissions arrangements as other schools, concerns have been expressed as to whether or not they have all been equally welcoming to pupils who have special educational needs. Whatever the truth of the matter, the academy in the final case study has well over 30 per cent of students with identified SEN, which is well above the national average. As well as a resource base for a dozen pupils with complex physical disabilities, there is a large provision in the form of a Student Support Centre for those with significant BESD.

The work of the Student Support Centre, which is described more fully later on, has developed a graduated system of rewards and sanctions. These are listed as a photocopiable resource on page 32, which other schools or services can compare with their own systems, and which may provide additional ideas.

The academy has developed a structural framework to show how the five outcomes of Every Child Matters are being pursued across the whole school. This is provided as a photocopiable resource (see page 34), so that schools can use it as a basis for discussing the development of their own blueprints.

Case study: The City Academy, Bristol

The academy caters for 1320 students between the ages of 11 and 18 years. It opened in 2003, initially using the buildings of the school it replaced, but in September 2005, the school moved into spacious new accommodation. The academy has specialist sports status. As the largest school in the area, it acts as a lead partner for post-16 provision, working with five other schools. Most of the students come from the surrounding area, which is one of social disadvantage. An above average number are entitled to free school meals, a large number are asylum seekers or refugees, and the majority are from ethnic minority groups.

More than a quarter of the students have some degree of learning difficulty or disability and over 40 have statements of special educational need. The school has a resource base for 12 students with complex physical disabilities, half of whom are wheelchair users. All of them are fully integrated into classes, but have teaching assistant support if needed and a room they can go to if they need a break from the classroom. There is a physiotherapy room and a physiotherapist visits every two weeks. A teaching assistant has also been trained to help with the students' physiotherapy programmes.

The Student Support Centre, for those with severe BESD, can cater for 120 students at a time. There are five tiers of support, as well as catering for internal exclusions, to try to prevent students having to be excluded altogether from the school. Detailed procedures are in place for monitoring progress, with the aim of reducing the tier of support the pupil needs. (An explanation of the tier system is provided on page 33).

Ray Priest, the Principal, believes that:

Every young person has a talent; there isn't a person on this planet who hasn't got an ability and a talent. I don't think we are always very good at recognising it. One of the things the academy's programme is doing, very successfully, is being able to really look, in an innovative way, at the curriculum and draw out the talents of young people.

The SENCO, Shirley Stevenson, is known as the Director, Every Child Matters. The school's Policy for Additional Needs is reviewed annually by an ECM Monitoring Group and the ECM Governor.

The out-of-hours programme has a wide range of clubs, activities and educational visits, with a balance of sports, music and drama. More than a thousand adult learners attend courses on the site.

Rewards	Sanctions
Verbal praise	Warning x3
Academy points	Moved within room
Good score on monitoring card	Negative score on target card
Positive event log	Temporary transfer to SSC Manager
Good day certificate	Negative event log
Phone call home	15-minute detention
Reward session in SSC	Phone call home
Top scorer £2 tuck voucher	30–60 minutes in detention
Letter home	Letter home
Monthly trip out	SLT involvement
Learning hero award	Internal exclusion
Visit to Principal	External exclusion
	Saturday/INSET detention

At the end-of-module celebration assembly, the following are celebrated:

■ Movement down a tier

■ The first, second and third highest scorer on target

Figure 2.5 The City Academy, Bristol, Student Support Centre, rewards and sanctions
Every Child Included, Paul Chapman Publishing © Rona Tutt, 2007

Tier	Provision	Referral	Criteria	Monitoring
1	Groupwork, eg anger management, anti-bullying etc Time out/keep calm card Watchful eye Sanctuary	SAC PLC SLT …at SSC programme leaders' discretion	Concerns raised via SAC/PLC/SLT/SSC	SAC/PLC/SSC informs parents End of group report shared and filed
2	Daily monitoring Rewards Occasional withdrawal Weekly phone calls Sanctuary Time out/keep calm card	Via ISAG …at SSC programme leaders' discretion	Child at school action at least Previous support tried Difficulties are seen daily and across a number of areas	SSC informs parents Logged SSC keeps records and monitoring Weekly contact home
3	As for tier 2 plus: Groupwork Withdrawal from up to 3 lessons (sometimes time limited) In-class support	Via ISAG …at SSC programme leaders' discretion	Child at school action at least or new referral at school action plus, or statement for BSED Tier 2 support given but groupwork added Difficulties are seen daily in many areas	As for tier 2 plus: PLP written if SAP or statement Meetings with parents/other agencies involved End of group report shared and filed
4	As for tier 3 plus: Withdrawal for 4 or more lessons Alternative provision	Via ISAG …at SSC programme leaders' discretion	Child at school action plus or statement for BSED Difficulties are seen daily across all areas	As for tier 3 plus: PLP written
5	Personal Support Plan SLT/Governors/LEA involvement	Following exclusion …at SSC programme leaders' discretion	Student at risk of permanant exclusion and/or not engaging with support in place	PSP written and regularly reviewed involving student, parents, SSC, SLT and other relevant parties

Figure 2.6 The City Academy, Bristol, tier stucture

Outcome	Lead	KS strategy	Whole school strategy	Operational management and monitoring	Responsibility for whole school delivery	Whole school provision map	Cross school direction	Additionality: provision map	Outside agencies	Community coordinator	Government key outcomes
Be healthy		V I	V I	• PSHE co • Head PE • Catering manager	• LFs • Catering team • PE team • PSHE teachers	• Venue catering • PSHE; sex and drugs • Food curriculum • PE lessons • LF time		• Counselling x 4 • LM • SSC groups • Disabled sport • KS4 life skills • Medical coordinator • Care plans	• S. nurse • S. doctor • S&L • Physio • OT • CAMHS • LEA PSHE advisor	E X T E N D	Lowering teenage pregnancy rate
Stay safe	P R I N C I P	C E	C E P R	• SACs • PLs • Estates manager • CP des teachers	• Attendance team • Teachers • Estate team • LFs	• safe buildings • classroom management • PSHE: sex and drugs • CP procedures • Access • Behavioural procedures	D I R E C T O	• SSC sanctuary • SSC bullying progs • LSAs • Att officer • KS4 life skills • LM	• Soc Ser • BASE • Police • Right Track • YIP • YOT	E D S C H O O	LoweringCp re-reg Achieving LAC placements
Enjoy and achieve	A L	I N C U P A L S	I N C U P A L S Sport	• PLs • SACs	• Teachers • LFs • Attendance co • Community personnel • BAT	• Classroom teaching • Celebrations • Rewards • Attend system	R E C M	• Development groups • SSC monitoring • 1:1 learning support • LM • LSAs • G&T activities	• EP • ASD team • LEA advisors • PLCs • Inclusion Links • Offsite prov	L S &	Increased school attendance Educational achievement of LAC
Make a positive contribution				• SACs • SEALs co • SV co • Leadership Co • PL BV/Cit	• Cit teachers • LFs • SV co • Leadership co	• SV forum • Village comps • Seals curric • Citizenship curric • Arts & Culture curric • Peer mentoring		• SV special • Young Bristol • Disabled forum • LAC focus	• YIP • YOT • ELAC • Youth Service	E M A P	Reduced levels of youth offending and school exclusions
Achieving economic well-being		K S 3 & 4	Curric Business	• PSHE co • Business leader • Wider part prog co	• Connexions • Community personnel • WP co • SACs • Y11/post 16	• Work related activities • Business links • WEX • University procedures • PSHE curric		• Skills for working life • Young Ent • Off site prov • Post 16 focus	• Business partners • HE partners		16–18 year olds in education employment and training

Figure 2.7 City Academy Bristol. A structural framework for pursuing the 5 outcomes of ECM

P *Every Child Included*, Paul Chapman Publishing © Rona Tutt, 2007

34

Successful strategies

- Ensuring that students are rewarded regularly, as well as applying sanctions when appropriate

- Having a tiered response to pupils' behavioural difficulties, so that the greater their need, the more support they will receive

- Minimising external exclusions by having a system for internal exclusions, when students are supervised on the premises but away from their peers

- Providing students with physical disabilities with the staffing and accommodation they need to be fully included, while ensuring they receive specialist support in terms of equipment and therapy

- Designing a structural framework to make sure the five outcomes of ECM are visibly embedded in the work and life of the school, including how the school is linking with outside agencies

---

Points to ponder

What do you see as the value of resourced provision?

Do you think there are particular types of needs that can benefit from it more than others?

Do you think there is scope for developing some form of resourced provision in your own school?

If your own school already has some form of resourced provision, how would you like to see it developing?

Addressing inclusion in the mainstream context

From the examples given in this chapter, it is clear that mainstream schools are constantly adapting what they do to address the needs of individuals with SEN, including the needs of those who may be outside their previous experience. There is a readiness to try out new methods and approaches and to engage with a wide range of staff in order to make sure all pupils in the school feel that they are genuinely included. There is no argument about whether or not the vast majority of pupils with SEN should be educated in mainstream schools. They have always been there and rightly so. The efforts mainstream schools have made to include more pupils with a diversity of needs should be recognised and applauded. Most of them have shown a remarkable capacity to be both flexible and resilient, as illustrated by the schools in the case studies and many more like them. As more pupils are included, however, it raises the question about what percentage of pupils with SEN it is either possible or appropriate to include. The growing number of resourced schools has been a welcome development, creating, as it were, a halfway house between pupils being in mainstream classes and being placed in a special school. As noted earlier, Ofsted inspectors have been impressed by what this type of provision is achieving for its pupils.

In trying to address the question of the roles of various kinds of provision and who they are for, it may be helpful to think first in terms of the age of the children and young people, and then at the different kinds of needs pupils have. Perhaps the first point to be made is that the younger the child, the easier it may be to include him or her in an environment geared to the needs of the majority, without having to make significant changes. Although there were a small number of children that the children's centre, for instance, found challenging, there was no question of not including them, but rather of having sufficient staff to cope with their needs. At this stage, children will have a greater degree of choice over what activities they wish to pursue and so there is less pressure on them to conform. This makes it easier for them to manage and for the pre-school environment to take a flexible approach. The head teacher of the children's centre said that when the children left the centre to start statutory schooling, there would be a few who would, from time to time, transfer to one of the special schools in the area. Both the first school and the girls' secondary school have links with special schools, so that they can, on occasions, have an exchange of pupils. This, in itself, heralds quite a change. It was not long ago that special schools and mainstream schools often moved in separate circles and the idea of being able to support each other was not common. Now, there is greater appreciation and knowledge of each other's work.

While all three schools (as opposed to the children's centre), felt able to include almost any child, they agreed that there were the occasional exceptions. This moves the discussion on to the second point about the nature of the difficulties pupils were experiencing. The head of the girls' school felt that those whose cognitive abilities lay right outside the usual range might themselves feel more included in an environment geared to their needs. Both the girls' school and the academy had put in place a variety of measures to support those with behavioural difficulties and those who had become disaffected, but they would occasionally pass students on to a pupil referral unit if that seemed more suited to their needs. In other words, having a range of provision helped to accommodate a small proportion of pupils where fitting into the mainstream environment did not necessarily seem to be the best option, either for them or for their peers.

A further challenge for mainstream schools in including the widest possible ability range, has been the pressure on schools to deliver in terms of test and examination results. As Rita Cheminais says in the Introduction to her book, *Closing the Inclusion Gap*:

> There also exists a dichotomy between measuring educational outcomes in terms of narrowly focused examination and test results, and including in mainstream schools children whose achievements are not recognised in national school performance tables. (Cheminais, 2003: ix)

Addressing Every Child Matters in mainstream schools

The more complex school populations become, the more necessary it is for the services that support children and families to work closely together. Children's centres are set up to make this joint working easier to achieve, by education, health and social care having a presence on the same site. This gives maximum support to parents and their children when they most need it. Schools, too, are moving in this direction, although the structures are taking longer to put in place. The academy's framework showing how the five outcomes of ECM are being pursued, for instance, gives an impressive array of links with outside agencies with which the school is involved. The five outcomes themselves are being very much embedded in the work of all schools. Tuckswood's overview of its School Improvement and Development Plan provided an example of how the outcomes are linked to the way the school wishes to develop.

The move to giving pupils more say in the running of their school was apparent throughout, whether through the approach to bullying or the move to class and school councils. The need to recognise the voice of the child is very strong. Pupils have a perspective on their experiences that adults can only guess at, unless the trouble is taken to ask them for their views and let them know that they can influence the way a school is run. Likewise, the move to seeing parents as partners in their child's education and helping them to become fully involved has a much higher profile than used to be the case. This is particularly relevant in the case of parents of children with SEN, who will require additional support, with the school and home working together to overcome the child's barriers to learning, whenever this is possible.

Children's centres are a prime example of how to provide education and childcare, how to open up the facilities for longer hours and how to make them available to the community as a whole. These are new roles for many schools, but they are responding in a variety of ways, from breakfast clubs to after-school clubs, from homework clubs to clubs for learning languages, playing sport or learning a musical instrument, and from parenting classes to lifelong learning for all. Schools cannot be accused of standing still, whether it is finding creative ways of addressing pupils' needs, or changing the way the entire school operates in order to take on the Extended Schools agenda. All types of schools, whether mainstream or special, are having to change out of all recognition. In this chapter, the role of mainstream schools in meeting the needs of children and young people with SEN has been considered. In the next chapters, the work of special schools will be looked at, so as to investigate their contribution to a flexible continuum of provision.

Points to remember

Children's centres and mainstream schools have adapted successfully to meet a much wider range of needs. These include:

- Young children from deprived or disorganised backgrounds who require an opportunity to develop the skills they need in order to be ready for school

- Children where the severity of their needs would previously have placed them in a special school

- Students whose disaffection or challenging behaviour have caused schools to widen their approaches, both providing very clear structures for some, and more flexible curriculum delivery for others. The role of resourced provision was considered as part of the flexible continuum of provision the government wishes to put in place.

At the same time as including pupils with a wide variety of needs, schools are changing to take on board the ECM agenda: working with a greater range of professionals (which is particularly necessary in supporting pupils with SEN) and extending what the school offers to its pupils, its families and to the wider community. Schools are also looking at various ways of embedding the five outcomes of ECM in everything they do.

TEN TIPS FOR BEST PRACTICE

1 Take note of the family context

2 Be prepared to explore new approaches

3 Try out new ways of working

4 Make SEN integral to the work of the school

5 Utilise the skills of the whole team

6 Use the community, including parents, as a resource

7 Discover what rewards motivate pupils

8 Reward more than punish

9 Listen to the voice of the child

10 Keep the five outcomes at the forefront of people's thinking

Final thoughts

- Do you think schools should play a part in the development of children's centres, or do you think they are better placed on their own campuses?

- Looking at the population of your own school, how do you think it has changed?

- Are there pupils who you think might feel more included in another provision, or would you like to feel that your school can provide for all the pupils who wish to attend?

- In what ways has your school become an extended school? What else do you feel it could provide?

 Recommended Reading

Gibson, S. and Blandford, S. (2005) *Managing Special Educational Needs.* London: Paul Chapman.

Hayward, A. (2006) *Making Inclusion Happen – A Practical Guide.* London: Paul Chapman.

Ofsted (2006) *Inclusion: Does It Matter Where Pupils are Taught? Provision and Outcomes in Different Settings for Pupils with Learning Difficulties and Disabilities.*

CHAPTER 3

Day special schools, federations and co-located schools

This chapter examines the changing role of special schools and how outreach work, federations and co-locations are helping to break down the divide between the special and mainstream sectors. It continues the discussion about the changing nature of the school population and considers which pupils may benefit from being placed in a special school. Case studies of schools include:

- A school for pupils with SLD, co-located with a mainstream school and part of a wider federation

- A school for the blind and visually impaired co-located with two mainstream schools, and a nearby school for the physically disabled

- Four special schools in Northern Ireland sharing a campus with one mainstream primary school

- A large generic special school in Wales, which has several discrete departments, including an eco centre.

The special school perspective

The previous chapter explored some of the diverse and creative ways mainstream schools have found of rising to the challenge of adapting what they do to provide for a wider range of needs. The chapter looked at what has been happening from the mainstream perspective, which was an appropriate place to start, given that the vast majority of pupils with SEN have always been educated in their local schools. Travelling along the continuum of provision to consider how best to provide for pupils whose needs are generally seen as more complex, this chapter moves on to consider recent developments from the special school perspective. This is not to say that the chapter is only about special schools, but the focus switches to looking at how special schools are adjusting to face fresh challenges, both in terms of the changing needs of *their* pupils and in terms of reaching out to form links with mainstream schools and colleges, as part of a newer dual role.

As the next chapter also takes a special school perspective, it may appear that undue attention is being given to a very small sector. There are two reasons for this approach. The first is that the work of this sector and the developments that are taking place within it are less well known. Ever since the Warnock Report and the 1981 Education Act, books have been written about how to make mainstream schools more inclusive (two recent examples are Anne Hayward's *Making Inclusion Happen*, and *Managing Special Educational Needs* by Suanne Gibson and Sonia Blandford). Very few have been devoted to what is happening in special schools. A notable exception is *Celebrating the Special School*, which was written by Michael Farrell in 2006, precisely because so little existed in the field. In the preface to his book, Farrell writes:

> *Far too little is said about the crucial work that special schools perform . . . good special schools up and down the country steadfastly continue their work, unnoticed, unsung and sometimes derided by those who have no conception of what a modern special school is like. (Farrell, 2006:v)*

The second reason is that, in order to illustrate the whole range of provision, the following chapter concentrates on the place of residential provision, which serves pupils who are mainly at the other extreme of the SEN continuum from those who are supported in mainstream schools. The contribution of such schools adds another dimension to the development of an inclusive education service.

Questions for reflection

- What role do you think special schools should play in a continuum of provision?

- Are there particular groups of pupils who you feel benefit more than others from being in a special school?

- Do you think there should be more pupils or fewer than there are now who go to special schools?

- Can you think of some of the ways in which you would like to see mainstream and special schools working together?

Special schools and the numbers game

As outlined in the opening chapter of this book, for many years special schools had a rather uncertain future. Now that they are seen as being part of inclusion rather than outside it, the sector as a whole has gained a greater sense of stability. This is not to say that individual schools necessarily feel secure. Local authorities have very different views about what constitutes an appropriate range of provision and some schools continue to be under threat. Others are losing their identity in amalgamations, which may make for more viable schools in terms of numbers, but which can be an uncomfortable process, particularly if rushed or not taking on board fully the views of all stakeholders, including the staff involved. The issue of the percentage of children with SEN that special schools might be expected to take in the future was raised at the end of the last chapter. The question that has not been resolved beyond all doubt is whether or not there is to be a reduction in the number of pupils attending special schools.

In the Introduction to her book, *Closing the Inclusion Gap*, Rita Cheminais assumes that 'The national goal for inclusion is to continue to reduce the number of children being educated in segregated special provision.' She goes on to describe the role of special schools as one that will promote this aim:

> *Special schools need to be viewed as part of a progression towards inclusion: part of the inclusion community – acting as 'launch pads' for the delivery of more flexible and effective advice and support to mainstream schools. (Cheminais, 2003: x)*

This may not be an unreasonable assumption, given that it was written in 2003. At that time, there is no doubt that the government expected the population in special schools to continue to fall, as mainstream schools became more adept at dealing with a wider range of needs. In the SEN Strategy of 2004, *Removing Barriers to Achievement*, it was stated that:

> *The proportion of children educated in special schools should fall over time as mainstream schools grow in their skills and capacity to meet a wider range of needs. (paragraph 2.15)*

While it is clear that mainstream schools have indeed developed their expertise in order to meet the needs of pupils who present new challenges to them, the number of pupils in special schools has remained fairly static over the last four or five years, at around 1.2 per cent of the school population. The report by the House of Commons Education and Skills Committee, *Special Educational Needs* (2006) picked up conflicting messages about whether or not the government wanted numbers in special schools to drop. The committee queried specifically the apparent change from what the SEN Strategy, *Removing Barriers to Achievement* states and the evidence given by the DfES to the committee. In his oral evidence, Andrew Adonis, the Minister with responsibility for SEN, stated that the government would be 'content' if decisions made by local authorities resulted in the current 'roughly static position in respect of special schools', and that the government did not 'have a view about a set proportion of pupils who should be in special schools' (volume 1, paragraphs 77–79). The committee went on to report that it had noticed a similar shift in the policy of some of the leading disability charities, which it described as now taking a more pragmatic approach towards specialist provision.

All pupils in special schools have to have a statement and the distribution of children with statements according to government figures is shown in Table 3.1. This means that almost 60 per cent of statemented pupils are in mainstream education, 34 per cent are in maintained special schools and 5 per cent in non-maintained and independent schools.

Type of provision	Number of statemented pupils
Mainstream	131,486
Maintained special school	83,128
Resourced provision	19,592
NMISS*	11,560
Educated other than in school	3,249
Hospital schools and PRUs	2,148
Awaiting provision	1,174
Early Years setting	947
* Non-maintained and independent special schools	

Table 3.1 Provision made for pupils with statements (2005 figures)

Non-maintained and independent special schools (NMISS)

Non-maintained special schools are non-profit-making independent schools run by charitable trusts. They have to be approved by the secretary of state under the 1996 Education Act and may receive grants from the DfES for capital building work and equipment. However, most of their money comes from the fees they charge local authorities and parents.

Independent special schools do not receive grants, but are funded solely by fees paid by local authorities and parents, plus any funds they raise themselves. Independent schools are also approved under the terms of the 1996 Education Act. Local authorities may not place pupils in independent schools that are not approved, without the approval of the secretary of state.

A dual role for special schools

The future role of special schools is one where there is clarity and consistency in what has been said for some time. In the *Report of the Special Schools Working Group* (2003) that preceded the SEN Strategy, it was stated that:

> *In the coming years we see special schools as being, along with others, at the leading edge of the government's wider education agenda. We see them participating in the full range of government initiatives and at the forefront of the wider education agenda. . . . We see more head teachers and teachers choosing to join the sector because of the opportunities that are on offer, and because the sector is one with a secure and long-term future. (Executive Summary: paragraph 17)*

The report's focus on asserting that special schools have a positive and continuing role helped to counteract the uncertainty that special schools had lived through during the 1980s and 1990s. This more optimistic outlook was reinforced by the SEN Strategy, which outlined what the future role of special schools would be:

> *Some schools have felt threatened by the inclusion agenda and unsure about what role they should play in the future. We believe that special schools have an important role to play within the overall spectrum of provision for children with SEN – educating some children directly and sharing their expertise with mainstream schools to support greater inclusion. (paragraph 2.12)*

In other words, the role special schools are expected to fill is set out as a dual one, which is described in the following terms:

- To educate pupils at the more complex end of the SEN continuum

- To work closely with mainstream schools in meeting the needs of their pupils as well

The second aspect, while a new development for some special schools, has been undertaken by others for at least the last 20 years. A fuller explanation of outreach work in general is given in Chapter 5, as part of a consideration of the work of a range of support services.

The *Report of the Special Schools Working Group* outlined some of the ways in which special schools can support mainstream schools. It suggested the following:

1 Advice on teaching styles and access strategies for particular children and young people with SEN

2 Advice on assessment, learning objectives and programme planning

3 Modelling of specialist teaching approaches and the use of specialist resources

4 Advice on provision of differentiated teaching materials and resources

5 Advice on adapting the curriculum

6 Moderation of P-scale assessments undertaken in mainstream schools

7 Training for teaching assistants

8 Training in behaviour management at a range of levels

9 Deployment and management of teaching assistants in the classroom

The case studies of schools in this chapter are designed to give a flavour of some of the ways in which special schools are developing outreach work.

A changing population?

While the situation regarding future numbers in special schools may not be entirely clear, the government's most recent statement is that it would not mind if numbers stabilised around the figure of the last few years – which would mean that special schools continue to provide for about 1.2 per cent of the school population. One of the reasons for this shift could be a realisation that as the skills of teachers in mainstream schools are growing, a larger number of children with complex needs are appearing in the school and pre-school populations. Some of the reasons for this will become apparent during the case studies.

The previous chapter outlined some of the ways in which mainstream schools are having to adjust what they do to meet a wider range of needs and in this chapter and the next, the examples given will demonstrate that special schools, too, are having to acquire additional expertise to meet fresh challenges.

Ofsted acknowledges this shift in its report, *Inclusion: Does it Matter Where Pupils are Taught?* in which it states:

> The categories that still define some special schools no longer accurately describe the diverse needs of the school population. For example, schools designated as providing for moderate learning difficulties (MLD) usually have pupils with a variety of other needs as well, including severe language delay, ASD and BESD. Head teachers reported that schools for pupils with SLD and PMLD now have a larger PMLD population and a substantial number of pupils with extremely challenging behaviour. (Ofsted, 2006: 8)

Schools catering for the types of needs highlighted here are included in the case studies, starting with a school for pupils who have severe learning difficulties (SLD), where there is a growing number of pupils with profound and multiple learning difficulties (PMLD). The school is also part of a federation of schools and it has been recently co-located with a mainstream primary school.

Co-located and federated schools

An interesting development that has helped to break down barriers between schools and between sectors, and which has assisted the progress towards a system more inclusive of all its schools, is the growing number of ways in which schools are being encouraged to work together. There have always been informal arrangements between schools, but now there is a climate of greater collaboration, despite a conflicting pressure on schools to compete with each other in an era of targets, constant testing and the publication of achievement and attainment tables. Particularly encouraging for special schools has been the move to co-locate some of them with mainstream schools. Co-located schools are one very visible way of removing any barriers between the sectors and making it much easier for schools of all types to share their facilities, their pupils and their staff.

Co-location

This is a term used in connection with the growing number of special and mainstream schools who share a site. There is no single blueprint for co-located schools, which can take many forms including:

- Mainstream and special schools that share the same site but remain physically detached

- Mainstream and special schools that are joined physically in one of a number of different ways, so that they share part or all of a building

Although some co-locations involve one special and one mainstream school, co-locations may involve several schools.

When new buildings are needed, the opportunity to co-locate schools may be taken. This may be part of the Building Schools for the Future programme (BSF).

Co-located schools and other schools may be part of federations.

Building Schools for the Future programme

This government programme was started in 2004 and aims to rebuild or renew every secondary school in England over a 10–15-year period. A programme for renewing primary schools is also beginning, although it is a few years behind the secondary programme.

There is no separate programme for rebuilding special schools, but they are being included in many local authorities' plans. Solihull, for instance, was in Wave 1 of the programme and three special schools were included in its rebuilding of schools in the north of the borough, two of which have been co-located with a secondary school.

Federations come in many forms, but, again, as far as special schools are concerned, there has been a welcome move to include special schools as well as pupil referral units (PRUs) in many of the federations that are appearing.

Federations

Hard federations

One governing body for all the schools, established using Federations Regulations that came in with the 2002 Education Act. May have a single head teacher across the group of schools, or a chief executive.

Soft federations

Each school has its own governing body, but there is a joint governing/management group, with or without delegated powers, using Collaboration Regulations under the 2002 Education Act.

Loose collaborations

Each school has its own governing body and the group of schools meet informally on an ad hoc basis. There are no regulations; schools make their own arrangements.

Two examples of well-known federations involving special schools are:

1   The West Sussex Federation, which, since September 2004, has had a joint governing body for two special schools (one for pupils with MLD and one, a few miles away, for pupils with BESD). A mainstream secondary school for boys completes the federation.

2   The Darlington Village Federation, opened in April 2005 after years of planning. It consists of a primary school, an all-age special school and a secondary school, all under the same roof, with a chief executive coordinating the work of the three schools and one joint governing body.

The *Report of the Special Schools Working Group*, much of which found its way into the government's SEN Strategy, said:

> *The government's diversity agenda offers an important opportunity and we want special schools at the heart of new federations and clusters of schools. Special schools have a vast wealth of knowledge, skills and experience which, if harnessed, unlocked and effectively utilised in mainstream schools, can help ensure inclusion is a success. (DfES, 2003: Executive Summary, paragraph 6)*

The school in the next case study is an example of a school that is co-located and is also part of a federation.

A co-located special school for pupils with SLD

Schools for pupils who have severe learning difficulties (SLD), which, as has already been mentioned, are likely to have a growing population of pupils with profound and multiple learning difficulties (PMLD), might be seen as an unlikely choice for co-locating with a mainstream primary school. Yet, in practice, the two schools work very well alongside each other.

Baytree School in North Somerset is part of the Weston Federation, which is a federation of four secondary schools and two special schools. The head teachers of all the schools sit on the strategic management board and they are part of the strategic leadership team. Staff representatives take forward the various strands of the federation's collaborative work, under the headings: Learning and Teaching, Organisation, CPD, ITT and ICT. A number of task groups may feed into these strands. The campus where Baytree itself is situated consists of three elements:

1 Baytree School

2 A primary school for 420 pupils with a nursery for 54 pupils

3 A Community Learning Centre with a library, conference and meeting rooms, one-stop shop for North Somerset Council, sports facilities, a police base and a college IT centre.

The campus as a whole has an Operations Management Team, which consists of both head teachers and a community services manager. They are also part of the Campus Facility Management Committee.

As part of its work with other schools, Baytree has developed a particular expertise in using the P scales, as many of its pupils will be working at this level for much, or all, of their school career. Formally used in special schools, P scales are about to become mandatory in mainstream schools as well, which is another indication of how their populations are changing.

P scales

P scales (or levels) are a set of indicators for recording the achievement of pupils with SEN who are working towards the first level of the National Curriculum (the level otherwise described as 'W'). There is a P scale for every National Curriculum subject. The P scales are split into eight different levels with P1 being the lowest and P8 the highest. P1 to P3 are not subject specific, but are the levels at which pupils with PMLD may be working.

The school has developed a pre-admission multi-agency form, an example of which is provided after the case study on page 49. This can be photocopied and used by schools or services wishing to discuss developing a similar format. The multi-agency meetings are usually attended by representatives from across the services, such as the local authority's SEN officer, the educational psychologist, the Disabled Children's Team Manager from Social Care, the Specialist Community Nurse, the parents, the Head Teacher and other appropriate staff.

Case study: Baytree School, North Somerset

Baytree is a school for 67 pupils aged 3–19. Mainly a school for pupils with severe learning difficulties (SLD), it tries to meet the needs as well of those with profound and multiple learning difficulties (PMLD), challenging behaviour, health care needs and autistic spectrum disorders (ASD). About 20 per cent of the pupils are wheelchair users. A few with the most complex medical needs have to have one-to-one health care assistants trained in preserving life. The head teacher, Carol Penney, has noticed a significant change in the school's population, with far more in need of close medical supervision. The school has created a small memorial garden dedicated to children who have died.

In September 2004, Baytree moved from its former site into a co-located building with a new primary school being built to cope with an increase in numbers in the area. It hopes to become a specialist special school with the SEN specialism in 'Learning and Cognition'. The schools are intertwined, so that they share a front entrance and reception area. Although they have their own blocks of classrooms within the same building, the specialist rooms, hall, dining room and staffroom are shared, as are the playgrounds. Carol Penney says:

> *I was well aware of the advantages of co-location and I still feel the opportunities far outweigh the adjustments that have to be made, but I did not fully appreciate how, as a head teacher, I would have less autonomy. For instance, some decisions need to go through both governing bodies and this takes time. Now, I have learnt to adjust, but it meant coming to terms with a new style of leadership.*

The school remains an all-age school. Being linked to a primary school and being part of a federation of secondary schools means that there is a greater emphasis on all pupils having integration opportunities during their time at Baytree, rather than just pupils with particular strengths in a subject such as art or PE, which is what happened before. Whole classes of secondary aged pupils now have weekly sessions at one of the mainstream secondary schools in the federation.

In addition, the school buys in packages of support from other providers to run an increasing range of courses for older pupils such as the ASDAN awards (including the Transition Challenge and the Youth Award Scheme). Work experience is offered to those who can benefit. The 16–19 class has links with a nearby adult centre. Having so many community facilities close at hand has opened up many opportunities for teaching independence and life skills. Some students will leave by this age to attend one of the residential colleges that run courses for students with severe learning difficulties, others prefer to stay until they are 19.

The school's outreach work includes supporting pupils who are integrating, and delivering training to mainstream schools, for instance on P-scale assessments, where the school has built up considerable expertise. Having some joint facilities, including a joint staffroom, means that there is a natural flow of views and ideas between the staff of the two schools, to the benefit of all.

Successful strategies

- Discussing common approaches before coming together as a co-located school, so that problems are sorted out in advance

- Accepting that the style of leadership will be different and planning for reduced autonomy

- Making full use of the new arrangements by allowing staff to spend time in each other's schools, familiarising themselves with the levels pupils are working at and how high expectations, although relative, should be common for all pupils

- Involving staff in the work of the federation, so that the load is spread and all gain benefit from working alongside colleagues from other settings

- Utilising the opportunities of an extended campus to teach independence and life skills in a real but safe environment

Points to ponder

- What are the advantages and disadvantages of an all-age school:
  - ◆ for pupils at any school?
  - ◆ for pupils with SLD?

- List all the ways in which your school is involved with other schools. What other links do you think it might be useful to have?

- Are there any fresh ways in which you could draw on the resources of the local community for the benefit of your pupils?

Name.................................Date of Birth................Date of Meeting............

Need	Provision	Met by/unmet	Action
1 Autism Communication Danger awareness High anxiety levels Social interaction			
2 Challenging Behaviour Pica Running off Aggressive behaviour			
3 Physical Integration of sensory systems Fine motor skills			
4 Self-care/personal Eating disorder Parental concerns Dressing Toilet			
5 Medical Epilepsy			

P Figure 3.1 Baytree School, pre-admission multi agency form
Every Child Included, Paul Chapman Publishing © Rona Tutt, 2007

All-age and phased special schools

Many special schools, like Baytree, are all-age schools. This is partly because they have tended to have fairly small populations, so that encompassing all ages makes them more viable. It may also be partly that when they were established, secondary-aged pupils sometimes had a more primary-based model for delivering the curriculum – with the same teacher being with them for most of their lessons and with less of an emphasis on progress across all subjects. More special schools are now being split into primary and secondary schools, or, if they remain all-age, the school is divided into distinct departments. The two schools in the next example used to be on the same site. The one that has remained continues to be an all-age school for pupils with physical disabilities (PD), but with different departments for the various age groups. The school for the blind and partially sighted, has been split into two departments in different buildings, as a result of being co-located with three mainstream schools. The two schools continue to have links with each other.

The school for pupils with physical disabilities accepts some children with severe dyspraxia, because there is no other provision for them. This is a condition that is increasingly being recognised, rather in the same way that dyslexia fought to be seen as a separate condition. Both dyspraxia and dyslexia (together with dyscalculia and dysgraphia, which have not yet received the same degree of recognition), are different types of specific learning difficulty, where some areas of a child's ability to learn will be affected but not others. This contrasts with the global or general learning difficulties of a child with moderate, severe or profound and multiple learning difficulties.

Dyspraxia (Developmental Coordination Disorder)

Dyspraxia, sometimes known as Developmental Coordination Disorder (DCD), is chiefly a difficulty with organising movement. Gross and fine movements will be affected. Problems with gross motor skills will be revealed in a lack of balance and rhythm, poor posture, weak muscle tone, a clumsy, awkward gait and a tendency to bump into people and objects, or even to trip and fall easily. There may be poor integration of the two sides of the body and poor hand-eye coordination. Difficulties with fine motor skills will show up in poor manipulative skills, such as dressing, eating with a knife and fork, doing jigsaws and holding a pencil in the correct grip to produce neat writing. Hand dominance may be late in becoming established.

In some cases, there is difficulty in coordinating the muscles involved in speaking (sometimes called oral or verbal dyspraxia), leading to exaggerated movements of the mouth or poorly articulated speech.

Schools for pupils with physical difficulties used to have several children with average and above intelligence, but, increasingly, if the only obstacle to be overcome is one of physical access to a mainstream curriculum, such children are now in their local schools. Correspondingly, the cognitive ability level of PD schools has fallen, although the majority of pupils with PMLD will be in SLD schools, rather than PD schools, where the curriculum, and the way it is delivered, can more easily be adjusted to their level of cognitive functioning. Some more academically able pupils, who have deteriorating conditions, or who need a high level of nursing care, may continue to be in PD schools rather than in mainstream.

Wilson Stuart opened in 1902 as a school for cripples (an indication of how terminology has changed), and moved to its current premises in 1956, which was also the location for Priestley Smith, the school for the blind and visually impaired already mentioned. The school has become very active in the field of outreach work and has become a resource for local schools. Two photocopiable resources are provided of its work:

1   A copy of the referral form that a local school fills in if it wishes to access the outreach service for one of its pupils. This can be used as a starting point for other schools developing such a service, although the information the school needs to collect will clearly depend partly on the outreach service's focus.

2   A diagram of the role of an outreach teacher from the school. Placing the child at the centre, as ECM suggests, the diagram shows all the links that an outreach teacher is involved in and the importance of joining up services to a child, rather than seeing outreach in isolation. Schools and services may find it helpful to create their own model on similar lines, allowing for their own particular circumstances.

At this point, it may be helpful to remember that it is not just special schools that offer help to mainstream schools. Many of the latter are building up their own bank of expertise and they are beginning to offer this to other schools. There is enough work for everyone who wishes to contribute; the important point is to be conscious of the need to know what services are available and to work together in meeting the needs of schools and their pupils.

WILSON STUART OUTREACH SERVICE REFERRAL FORM

PLEASE RETURN TO;

Barbara Hunter,
Wilson Stuart Outreach,
Wilson Stuart School,
Perry Common Road,
Erdington,
Birmingham B23 7AT
Tel: 373-4475   Fax: 373-9842

Data Protection Act 1998 BCC Education Service, Wilson Stuart Outreach Service
The information requested on this form is required for the purpose of referring the above pupil to this service.
The information provided by you may be disclosed to other professionals working with this pupil for educational
purposes.

Please ensure that permission from the Parent/Carer has been obtained for this referral.

Parents/Carers signature

CHILD'S NAME...d.o.b..............

ADDRESS...YEAR.............

....

SCHOOL... School tel. no..........

ADDRESS...

....

HEAD TEACHER..

SENCO...CLASSTEACHER..................................

WHAT IS THE NATURE OF THE CHILD'S PHYSICAL/MOTOR DIFFICULTIES?
e.g. Cerebral Palsy, spina bifida, ?   If there is a diagnosis, please specify: ....

WHAT ARE THE MAIN AREAS OF CONCERN? (Please number according to priority)

Mobility/Access	...	Information/Communication Technology ...
Gross Motor Skills	...	Perceptual Skills ...
Self Help Skills	...	Handwriting ...
Organisational Skills	...	Fine Motor Skills ...
Other (Please specify)	...	

P Figure 3.2 Wilson Stuart School, referral form
Every Child Included, Paul Chapman Publishing © Rona Tutt, 2007

Details of Code of Practice Stage

Please enclose copy of current IEP

Who else is involved with this child? (Please specify)

Agency	Name
Ed. Psych.	
Medical Consultant	
Physiotherapist	
Occupational therapist	
PSS	
VTS	
Behaviour support	
Speech therapist	
Other	

STATEMENTED PUPILS

DOES THIS PUPIL HAVE ANY SUPPORT FROM A LEARNING SUPPORT ASSISTANT?   If so:

How many hours?   Name:..

DETAIL ANY OTHER BACKGROUND INFORMATION WHICH MIGHT BE RELEVANT?

Signed...Headteacher   Date....................................

....SENCO

....Class Teacher

2

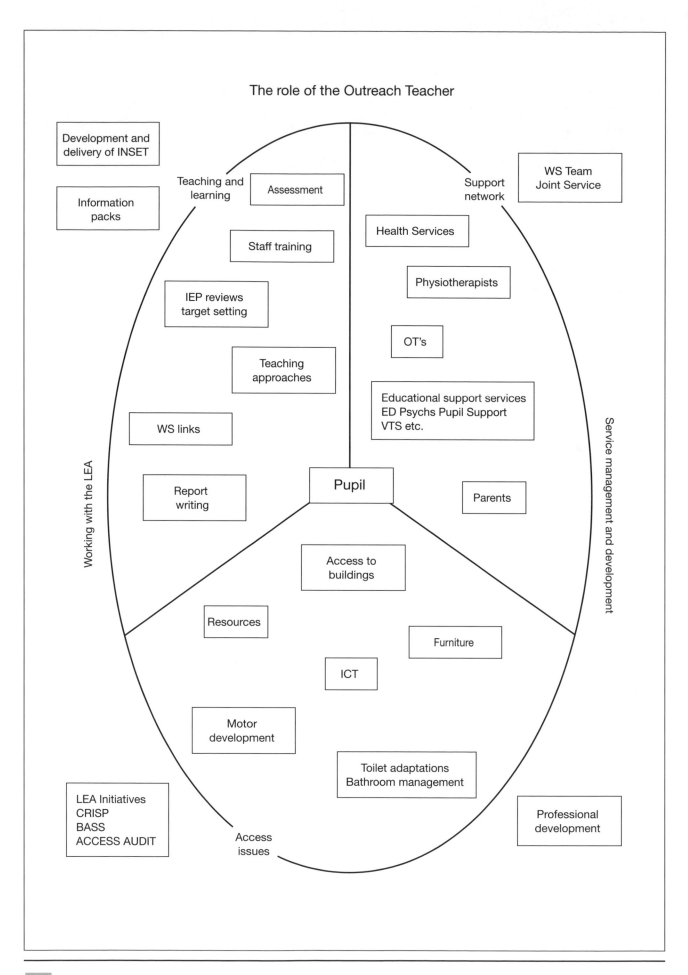

The role of the Outreach Teacher

Development and delivery of INSET

Information packs

Teaching and learning

Assessment

Staff training

IEP reviews target setting

Teaching approaches

WS links

Working with the LEA

Report writing

Support network

WS Team Joint Service

Health Services

Physiotherapists

OT's

Educational support services ED Psychs Pupil Support VTS etc.

Service management and development

Pupil

Parents

Access to buildings

Resources

Furniture

ICT

Motor development

Toilet adaptations Bathroom management

LEA Initiatives
CRISP
BASS
ACCESS AUDIT

Access issues

Professional development

Figure 3.3 Wilson Stuart School, the role of the outreach teacher
Every Child Included, Paul Chapman Publishing © Rona Tutt, 2007

Priestley Smith, the school for the blind and partially sighted, has also experienced a change in its population for similar reasons. Children with a visual impairment have more technological support to maximise any vision they may have. This has made it easier for many of them to be provided for in a mainstream environment. Some mainstream schools will have resourced provision for those with a sensory impairment and many local authorities will have advisory teachers, or visiting teachers, who specialise in this area and can advise schools. At present, visual and hearing impairment are the only conditions where there are mandatory qualifications that teachers have to obtain if they are working in this field for any length of time.

Mandatory qualifications for teachers of pupils with sensory impairments

Qualified teachers who take classes of pupils with:

- Hearing impairment (HI)

- Visual impairment (VI)

- Multi-sensory impairment (MSI)

must hold a relevant mandatory qualification. A number of courses are available, two of which are run in conjunction with special schools. The University of Birmingham runs courses for HI, VI and MSI, all of which lead to the relevant mandatory qualification.

The result of more children with sensory impairments being in their local schools is that special schools are likely to have the pupils who have other difficulties in addition to their visual impairment. It is often the combination of conditions that makes it harder for children to succeed in a mainstream environment. So, special schools, like mainstream schools, are experiencing the need to find ways of educating a more complex population.

Case study: Priestley Smith and Wilson Stuart Schools

Priestley Smith is a school for the blind and partially sighted. It can take 55 pupils aged 2–17. Since the school moved from its site with Wilson Stuart, it has been rebuilt and co-located with three mainstream schools. The Primary Department is housed between a new infant and a new junior school, which are all housed under the same roof. As pupils and staff walk down the central corridor, there is no indication of where each school begins and ends, but very much a sense of one building, within which each has its own facilities as well as areas that are shared. Pupils and staff can move freely between the different

▶

schools, allowing for a flow of pupils in and out of the specialist provision. The Secondary Department has been built as an additional wing to the secondary school that was already on the site and is just across the driveway from the primary schools.

The school offers a specialist curriculum, which has been developed to enable pupils to access the national curriculum and to gain the skills needed for a full adult life. This includes mobility training, touch-typing, Braille tuition and other augmentative media. On the staff are mobility officers, who are also qualified Living Skills Instructors. Medical services include an ophthalmologist, an ophthalmic optician and a dispensing optician who visits weekly. There is an Assessment Service for children aged 5–16, who are tested with and without low vision aids as well as being assessed on mobility. Outreach work is carried out in conjunction with the local authority's Visiting Teacher Service.

Wilson Stuart is a special school for 135 pupils aged 2–19 who have physical difficulties. An increasing number have additional needs, including severe learning difficulties or complex medical needs. A few have severe dyspraxia. There is a hospital school attached to it. The school achieved Beacon status before becoming the first school of its kind to be a specialist sports college. It is a hub school for the School Sport Coordinator Partnership programme, involving 30 primary and secondary mainstream schools. There are two full-time nurses, as pupils have increasingly complex medical problems. Over 50 per cent of its pupils are wheelchair users. The head, Anne Thompkinson, says that it is very noticeable that the younger pupils are more disabled, with some needing one-to-one medical care.

As the school covers a very wide age range, it is divided into separate departments, with 16–19 year olds studying at a local college, supported by staff from the school. There is a substantial outreach service to local schools. Pupils from both sectors can spend time in each other's schools.

Successful strategies

- Helping pupils to acquire the skills they will need to have a fulfilled life by providing them with full-time access to specialist teaching and resources, while giving them access to mainstream experience

- Working with the local authority in sharing the expertise built up in the special school, so that it can be of benefit to a wider group of pupils

- Making sure outreach work complements the work of other services and helps to build up the confidence of mainstream colleagues

- Using the setting to maximise opportunities for pupils to move between settings as appropriate

- Providing an assessment service to help in the identification of needs and to be part of the provision to meet those needs

---

Points to ponder

- What do you think are the advantages and disadvantages of special schools for those with physical disabilities?

- Would you give the same answer or a different one for those with visual impairments?

- How would you organise specialist provision for those with physical or sensory needs?

- If you could design co-located provision for your own school or area, what model would you go for?

Special schools in Northern Ireland

In Northern Ireland, the equivalent of the 1970 Education Act in England, that saw all children brought within the education service for the first time, did not come into effect until 1986. It is more recently that schools have been established for those at the lower end of the cognitive ability range. Although it is more usual to find one special school located with one or more mainstream schools, in Belfast there is a site where four special schools share a campus with one mainstream primary school. This has introduced some interesting work across the special schools, who are able to draw on each other's expertise and facilities. There is a smooth transfer of pupils from one special school to another and the children remain in familiar surroundings even when changing schools. Because it could be rather overwhelming for the one mainstream school (and the schools were grouped in this way because of vacant land, rather than as part of a strategic plan), many of the mainstream links have been formed with other schools nearby, rather than with the one on the campus.

Two of the special schools on the campus are for pupils with severe learning difficulties, and also have some pupils who have profound and multiple learning difficulties. One is a primary school and the other is a separate, but geographically close, secondary school. A third school caters for primary-aged pupils who have moderate learning difficulties. The fourth school, which was the only one on the site originally, is an-all age school for pupils with physical disabilities.

Case study: A group of special schools in Belfast

Oakwood School and Assessment Centre caters for around 100 pupils from 3–8 who have or are suspected of having SLD. The school also runs a pre-school support service, working with families identified by the Educational Psychology Service. As there is a growing number of pupils with ASD or PMLD, children are based in classes according to age and the nature of their difficulties, so a parallel stream exists for pupils with ASD and separate classes for children with PMLD. The school feels that this enables staff to give more specific help in meeting needs. The school has also developed a separate unit within the school for those with the most challenging behaviour. The school runs an ASD Advisory Service to local schools, which is housed separately on the campus, and managed by the school.

▶

Glenveagh School for older pupils with SLD takes 176 pupils aged 8–19, most of whom transfer from Oakwood, with a smaller group from Harberton, the MLD school on the same site. There are two separate classes for PMLD pupils and there used to be separate provision (as at Oakwood) for those with challenging behaviour, but this has been disbanded in favour of one-to-one support in class. There are four classes for older students which link with the local college and there is a deliberate attempt to make the students feel they are at college rather than at school. Courses include horticulture, bakery and car valeting. One class is for students with more complex needs, who follow a more active, outdoor curriculum, including the use of a nearby outdoor activity centre.

Harberton School is a primary school for 150 pupils with MLD. The school has developed into six discrete departments. Apart from the school itself, these are: a diagnostic nursery, a nursery support service (to support children in local nurseries), an outreach learning service, an outreach behaviour service and a reading unit for those with dyslexia. The head teacher reports a dramatic change in the profile of needs, with mainstream returners falling from 30 per cent to 4 per cent. Having pupils who need tube-feeding and others who have to be physically restrained also shows the changing nature of pupils' needs. (Further details of the different aspects of the school's work are given in Chapter 5.)

Fleming Fulton was the original school on what has now become a sizeable campus. It caters for 150 pupils aged 3–19 who have physical impairments and disabilities. Because of its age span, the school is divided into nursery, primary, and secondary departments. The ability range is from MLD upwards. At the age of 16, many stay on to complete a wide range of academic and vocational courses. The school has orthopaedic, physiotherapy and speech and language departments, as well as close links with social care. Several pupils spend time at one of two respite care homes available to their families. The school has many links with local schools and colleges, including grammar schools (to which some pupils have transferred) and other schools on the campus who use its medical facilities, which include a dental surgery and a large indoor pool. Pupils can also join in arts and music projects arranged by the school.

Successful strategies

- Providing assessment places for young children and also supporting children in their local nurseries

- Organising the school to address the needs of different groups of children within it

- Having contact with other special schools, as well as with mainstream schools and colleges

- Linking with social services to ensure that the school and respite care work closely together in supporting pupils and families

- Looking outwards to supplement the services available to local schools

---

Points to ponder

■ What do you see as the advantages and disadvantages of special schools being grouped together?

■ As special schools take on a more diverse range of needs, do you think children should be divided into classes by age, by need, or both?

■ What do you think are the most effective ways of supporting pupils with severe behaviour problems?

■ To what extent do you think special schools should take on a wider role?

Generic special schools

Some special schools have been very small; too small in some cases to provide a broad enough curriculum, or to give pupils enough of a peer group. In some cases, this has been addressed by amalgamating special schools, not necessarily with another school catering for a similar population, but rather a more generic special school. For instance, SLD schools have been combined with MLD schools, MLD with EBD, or sometimes all three together. In some places, such as Guernsey, where the population is more thinly spread, a new special school, Le Rondin, has been built to cater for all types of needs. In some areas, this may be the only answer, but there can be a danger that, in trying to meet a wider range of needs, no pupil's needs are properly addressed. The *Report of the Special Schools Working Group* commented on the move towards more generic special schools as follows:

> *The working group believes there may be scope for LEAs to organise and structure special school provision in a more differentiated way, so that particular schools specifically cater for children and young people with a particular mix of needs. This would allow special schools to tailor and target provision to meet each and every one of the child's needs. It would also allow staff working in special schools to develop more expertise and greater specialist knowledge of the area in which they are working. (DfES, 2003: paragraph 80)*

In other words, the working group was worried about the trend towards mixing pupils with different kinds of needs and wanted to encourage a return to a more traditional pattern of schools, each with its own specialism.

Wales is similar to England in that each local authority decides what specialist provision it will make for pupils with SEN. In the last reorganisation, when Wales went from having 8 local authorities to having 22, almost all opted to retain special schools, but, increasingly, as in England, where there is an opportunity to build, local authorities may be looking towards co-locating specialist provision with mainstream schools. (An example of a co-located school in Wales is given in the next chapter.) Jane Davidson, the Minister for Education for Wales, is supportive of the special schools sector and has provided funding to 'unlock the potential of special schools in Wales', including funding to support mainstream schools.

St Christopher's School in North Wales was originally an MLD School. In 2000, when it moved on to its present site (a former secondary school), it amalgamated with an SLD school. The head teacher, Maxine Grant, says: 'I wanted the school to be housed in a former comprehensive, because we strive to be like one.' She also believes in being a school that draws in the community. A conference room is being designed with video conferencing facilities, which will be available to the community. Adults with learning difficulties have their own accommodation in the school. After-school clubs run from 3.30 till 5 p.m. The fitness and PE centre is used by staff and the community in the evenings, and there is an evening class for the Duke of Edinburgh Award Scheme. Students from local schools attend some of the courses run by the school as part of its extensive 14–19 programme and over 50 students from St Christopher's follow courses in local schools.

The school also has a strong focus on the environment and has gained eco-school status. (A description of the school's Millenium Eco Centre is given in Chapter 5.) The grounds have been developed by the pupils and the flower beds and greenhouses are accessible to wheelchair users. In the allotment area, different surfaces have been created to help wheelchair users and others with mobility problems to get used to uneven surfaces when away from the school environment.

Successful strategies

- Making sure a wide variety of needs are met by having discrete departments within the school

- Achieving a less congested environment for all pupils by staggering break times and lunch breaks

- Encouraging students with behavioural difficulties to learn how to look after the environment, rather than destroying it

- Having close links with local schools for all ages and providing a purpose for them to have regular contact with the school

- Bringing the community into the school by running a number of facilities which benefit them as well as the pupils at the school.

Points to ponder

- How far do you think it helps to meet diverse needs if pupils are given the opportunity to work with others who have similar needs?

- Do you think that students who have behavioural difficulties can be helped to care for the environment by learning to look after it??

- How does your school encourage the community to come into the school? What else could you do to make local people feel that the school is part od the community??

Case study: St Christopher's School, North Wales

St Christopher's School caters for 230 pupils aged 5–19 years. Originally formed from the amalgamation of an MLD and an SLD school, the school caters for pupils with a wide range of difficulties. Due to its size, it has been able to form six distinct departments within the school:

- Junior, Middle and Secondary School Departments

- Independent Living Department for 14–19 year olds who follow both the national curriculum and a developmental curriculum that encourages them to acquire the skills for independent living

- Curriculum Enrichment Department, which is designed to cover college links, integration into mainstream schools, the school's hair and beauty salon, the car washing and valeting business, and the 14–19 curriculum. As part of this department's work, the local 14–19 partnership funds a curriculum enrichment programme, with college placements for students from all the secondary schools in the town, including some students from St Christopher's. St Christopher's coordinates this programme, with all pupils having the opportunity to gain OCN units, entry level and NVQ qualifications.

- Behaviour Support Unit which provides for 55 students from 6–19, some of whom have been in serious trouble outside the school. They have a separate entrance and start the day with breakfast at 8 a.m. The aim is to give them a clear structure and a sense of purpose, while allowing scope to develop individual talents, including sailing, canoeing, caring for the environment rather than destroying it, and joining in with the school's exam classes up to GCSE and AS Level

In addition, the school runs a café, a fair trade shop, and a hair and beauty salon, all of which are open to the public, and which the pupils help to run. This gives them the opportunity of gaining work experience and of acquiring qualifications at the same time. They also help to run a car wash and valeting service. The school runs a prefect system. There is a school council and a children's forum for the environment. One of the students represents special school pupils on the 'Funky Dragon', which is the children's section of the Welsh Assembly.

The school has an emphasis on caring for the environment and pupils over the age of 14 can join the Environmental Task Force, giving up one day a week to help look after the gardens of senior citizens, clearing paths and streams and cutting hedges. The school's Millennium Eco Centre is on a separate site and provides additional opportunities for students from the school and the locality to study the environment, horticulture and land management.

A school liaison officer (who is on the management team) has responsibility for a large number of children who have social workers, as well as the 30 children who are 'looked after' children. The school also has links with health care services through having speech and language therapists and physiotherapists who visit the school.

A poem called 'Memories' is included below because it was written by a pupil from this school, and like the other two poems in this book, was published in *'Like everyone else . . .'*, NASEN's (2006) collection of poems in inclusion.

Memories

It's hard to forget the past when so much
has happened to me
Before the illness happened I was full of
glee.
I used to be an acrobat and a tap dancer
too,
Now Eleanor is placing her footsteps in
the things I used to do.

People look at me differently in my
wheelchair,
But what they don't know is this
I used to dance and skip and ride my bike
And do so many things I used to like.
I still have these memories sweet
Remember these words when we happen to
meet.

K. Clays, age 18, St Christopher's School, Wrexham

Addressing inclusion in the special school context

In the last chapter, inclusion was considered from the mainstream perspective and examples were given of some of the ways in which mainstream schools have adjusted to cater for a far wider range of pupils than used to be there. This chapter has focused on inclusion from the special school perspective and it is interesting to note how some of the issues are the same, in particular the changing population.

It was apparent from the case studies, that regardless of the type of special school, all schools felt they had had to adjust to pupils they had not previously encountered. Some did this by integrating their populations; others by having discrete classes or departments within their schools, where they felt they could target the support children needed more directly. Although none of the schools were specifically for pupils with behavioural difficulties, like the mainstream schools in the previous chapter, the growing presence of children with BESD was having an effect on the organisation of the school, either in terms of needing more staff for one-to-one support, or in deciding to run separate classes, or even departments, to accommodate their needs and those of the rest of the school. As one deputy head teacher remarked:

> *We needed to let the rest of the class get on. Their progress was being affected by pupils who were disruptive and they are, after all, children who have their own difficulties.*

Some might suggest that this could be seen as taking a less inclusive approach, but this need not be the case. It is not a question of taking a child out of a class just to enable the rest of the class to learn. None of the schools, whether mainstream or special, used a different environment (or, indeed, one-to-one support in class), as a punishment, but as a means of making it easier for pupils to receive a high level of support, and to be in an environment where their behaviour was less likely to inhibit their ability to learn. Although the nature of the needs of their pupils may be different, some SLD schools have responded to the increase in pupils with PMLD, by creating separate classes for them, so that there is the time, space, staffing and equipment to support their very considerable physical and intellectual needs.

As well as the alteration in their populations, another major change for special schools has been the growing emphasis on a dual role, whereby they share with mainstream schools some responsibility for the wider group of children who have SEN. In the last chapter, it was clear that links between mainstream and special schools are increasing and that many will have contact with each, partly to accommodate the needs of pupils who may benefit from some time in both environments. From the special schools' point of view, new avenues have opened up with the encouragement to work in partnership in a number of ways, whether through federations, co-locations or working together on specific strands of the curriculum, such as courses for 14–19 year olds.

A further extension of these links is the encouragement for special schools to provide outreach services to local schools. Outreach takes many forms, which will be discussed more fully in Chapter 5, but whatever form it takes, it is helping to bring schools together in supporting children with SEN.

Addressing Every Child Matters in special schools

Special schools have always had greater involvement with other services because of the nature of their children's needs. Many of them require ongoing medical support and a range of therapies, particularly speech and language therapy, occupational therapy and physiotherapy. A higher proportion of their families will be known to social services, because of the need for respite care and other forms of family support. An above-average number of children in care are also to be found in special schools, because the turbulence of their backgrounds and disrupted lifestyles will have exacerbated any learning difficulties or, indeed, helped to create them. Putting the child and family at the centre of what a school does is easier when dealing with smaller numbers. Parents may feel more in need of support from the school because their children are more dependent for longer and in some cases for ever, and there may be more concerns about their progress and well-being, which need to be shared and discussed.

On the other hand, day special schools have a greater problem than mainstream schools when it comes to developing extended hours. Because most pupils rely on transport being provided, it is less straightforward to change the hours of the school day, or to have pupils who normally travel together wanting to attend clubs on different days or at different times. A further complication is that the special schools pupils attend may be some distance from their home community, so the question arises as to whether they stay on at their own school, or participate in clubs and activities nearer home. These considerations have meant that some special schools have concentrated on running lunch-time clubs, rather than ones that interfere with transport. However, others, as evidenced by some of the case studies, are extending their days at both ends and widening the range of activities they offer.

Again, because of their pupils coming from a wide area, special schools have sometimes been seen as more detached from the local community than other schools. That is changing, whether through outreach work, linking with other schools and colleges to provide courses, or welcoming the community into the school to attend activities. As Farrell notes, many people have little idea of what the special school of today looks like. Certainly, it is very different from the special school of even a decade ago. Despite uncertainty over their futures, head teachers and their staffs in special schools have shown the same spirit of adaptability, enterprise and resilience as their mainstream colleagues. The extraordinarily exciting and varied range of their current work has been demonstrated by the examples in this chapter, and will be followed up further in the next chapter when special schools with residential accommodation are considered.

Key points

While the exact size of the future special school population has been queried, it is possible that it could remain at about its present size. Special schools, like mainstream schools, are coming to terms with children whose needs are different from previous intakes and increasingly complex. They have addressed this in different ways; some schools remain all-age, others are phased; some are more generic, others concentrate on particular needs.

In the other aspect of their dual role, special schools are to be responsible for educating children with complex needs while, *at the same time*, having a wider role in working with mainstream schools to meet the needs of the majority of such pupils who remain in their local schools. The advent of federations, co-located schools and other forms of collaborative working, are helping to create a more flexible range of provision, as well as encouraging all schools to share their experience and expertise.

Special schools are a small but significant part of an inclusive system. They are developing an extended role in a number of imaginative ways. Being smaller communities, they have more easily been able to put individual children and their families at the heart of what they do.

Final thoughts

- Do you think your view of special schools has changed while reading this chapter? Is it more positive or negative than it was before?

- How would you like your school or service to contribute to breaking down the barriers between the sectors?

- Do you think it can be true that both mainstream and special schools are seeing more complex children?

TEN TIPS FOR BEST PRACTICE

1 Make links with the schools around you

2 Integrate your school into the community

3 Decide how the school should be structured to meet fresh challenges

4 Eliminate preconceptions and focus on individual needs

5 Become actively involved in federations, collaborations or partnerships

6 See pupils with BESD as a challenge rather than a problem

7 Stagger break times and lunch breaks to cut down on conflict

8 Interest pupils in nurturing the environment

9 Set up a club or activity for those with unusual interests

10 Discuss what direction outreach work could take

 # Recommended reading

Cheminais, R. (2003) *Closing the Inclusion Gap: Special and Mainstream Schools Working in Partnership.* London: David Fulton.

Farrell, M. (2006) *Celebrating the Special School.* London: David Fulton.

Department for Education and Skills (2003) *The Report of the Special Schools Working Group.* Nottingham: DfES Publications.

CHAPTER 4

Special schools with residential provision

This chapter covers special schools that are partly or mainly residential. Using the case studies of four schools to illustrate innovative practice, it considers:

- The different types of residential provision and the role of boarding placements

- The kinds of needs and personal circumstances that may require this degree and type of support

- The particular ways in which schools with residential provision have addressed inclusion and Every Child Matters

Why have residential provision?

State boarding schools for pupils who do not have SEN are comparatively rare. There are, however, several maintained special schools that offer some boarding provision. In addition, there are many special schools that are independent or non-maintained schools. Some of these are run by charities that own a single school (Sunfield, which is described later in this chapter is an example of a charity running one school), and some, such as the National Autistic Society or SCOPE (the disability organisation in England and Wales whose focus is people with cerebral palsy), that have several schools.

There are two main reasons why pupils with special educational needs may need to board:

1 The distance pupils have to travel to reach a school that can give them an appropriate education means that attending daily may not be a sensible option

2 The nature of the pupils' difficulties means that a) they are helped by having a 24-hour curriculum, b) the family is unable to support them, or c) both of these situations apply.

The more complex the child's needs, the more likely it is that he or she will require some residential provision. The case studies in this chapter reveal that special schools with a residential element are addressing the same issues as other types of schools, namely:

- Adjusting to meet the needs of changing populations

- Adapting to meet new expectations in the light of the SEN Strategy and the ECM Agenda findings

- Reaching out beyond the institution to form links with other educational establishments and with the local community

As costs have risen, interest has increased in finding ways of cutting back on the expense of boarding provision, particularly if it is 'out-authority' provision. This term is used in two ways. Generally, it is used to describe a school that is situated in a different authority to the one in which a pupil lives. The child, therefore, is being sent out of his or her own authority to access provision that is available elsewhere. The term can also be used to describe provision that is situated in the authority where the pupil lives, but is not run by that authority. It may, for instance, be a non-maintained or independent school that is local to the child, but will not be managed by the local authority.

Questions for reflection

- Do you think boarding provision may be the best arrangement for some pupils with SEN? If so, which children should benefit?

- If not, what other arrangements do you think might be made for pupils with more complex needs?

The distance factor

The first reason given for residential provision was that of distance. The following case studies are of two schools that offer both boarding and day provision, primarily because their pupils come from a very wide area. They are very different, however, in the type of students they educate.

Educating pupils with autistic spectrum disorders (ASD)

The first example is of a school in Wales for pupils with ASD, some of whom have Asperger's syndrome. There is a large measure of agreement that Asperger's syndrome is part of the autistic spectrum. Pupils with this diagnosis are generally at the more able end of the spectrum, whereas those with 'classic autism' are likely to have severe or moderate learning difficulties in addition to their autism. 'High-functioning autism' is a term that is used less often, but it generally indicates people who are nearer to those with classic autism in terms of the severity of their condition, but similar to those with Asperger's syndrome in terms of their cognitive ability.

The autistic spectrum

Severe learning difficulties　　　　*Moderate learning difficulties*　　　*Average and above*

Classic autism　　　　　　　　　　　High　functioning　autism

Asperger's syndrome

As the head teacher, Dr Michael Toman, intended his school to develop as a regional resource, he knew this meant avoiding being geared either to the more able end of autism or to the more severe end, and organising the school so that all degrees of autism and cognitive ability could be catered for. Classes are designed so that a separate curriculum can be offered to those with the most complex needs, while at the more able end of the ability range, pupils benefit from being able to join mainstream classes and having access to GCSE Exams.

As mentioned in the case study of St Christopher's School in the previous chapter, Wales, like England, is seeking to co-locate schools when the opportunity arises, and Ysgol Plas Brondyffryn is a case in point. The school is just settling into its new buildings, opening up a much wider range of opportunities for its pupils to mix with those in mainstream schools, and for the mainstream schools to benefit from some of the facilities and experience of the special school. Indeed, the school has changed out of all recognition, from being a small, secluded school tucked away in a manor house, to an outward-looking establishment that is fully in touch with the community and, as a regional resource, shares its knowledge of ASD with a much wider audience.

Case study: Ysgol Plas Brondyffryn

Ysgol Plas Brondyffryn in Denbighshire caters for 125 pupils aged 3–19 who have ASD. In 2000, the school gained the support of the Welsh Assembly in having a role as a Regional Centre for Autism. There is boarding accommodation for 24 pupils, who are in residence for two or four nights a week. Although the main reason for boarding is one of distance, a small number of children are in care (where part-time boarding makes it easier to find a foster family who can cope), and as older students reach adolescence, a 24-hour curriculum helps some of them learn how to manage their behaviour in a variety of social situations and to develop independence.

The residential accommodation is separate from the educational side and occupies part of a former hospital site, which is situated in spacious grounds on the edge of the town. Some of the wards have been imaginatively transformed into a series of self-contained flats. The children live in family groupings. They help to plan the menus, go into town and buy the ingredients for their meals, as well as taking part in clubs and other activities in the locality.

▶

The school is about to register as a children's home, so that it can accommodate a small but increasing number of pupils with autistic spectrum disorders for whom 52-week placements are being sought. A separate building on the same campus as the other children who board has been prepared for up to 12 of these most challenging pupils. A suite of classrooms is being created close by with 3 classes of 4 students each, all of whom will have one-to-one support.

Both the primary and secondary parts of the school have recently been co-located, so that they physically adjoin a mainstream primary and a high school respectively, sharing some of the facilities. The new buildings are strikingly modern and unusual in design. For instance, the secondary department has been built at an angle to the high school, so as to create a large internal triangular courtyard area, for pupils who prefer to be in a more enclosed space.

There is an inclusion and assessment class for children of nursery and reception age, who attend their local schools on a part-time basis. The primary pupils mix with the mainstream school pupils for lunchtimes and playtimes. Pupils with more limited cognitive ability have lunch in their classrooms and stay with their own teacher as they get older, rather than having a secondary-style curriculum.

The secondary department has forged strong links with the high school to which it is attached and its integration programme enables some students to transfer to mainstream education. Some students take ASDAN awards, others entry level qualifications or GCSEs. There is a separate Post-16 provision for up to 15 students, linked to the local community college.

The school has very good relationships with professionals working in health and social care. Student nurses, doctors and other health professionals have benefited from attachments to the school.

Michael Toman has found that personal contact with professionals from the different services works extremely well. Difficulties that arise are more at the level where decisions have to be made on issues such as funding. For instance, there is sometimes a debate about pupils who are in residence and whether they are there as a form of respite care (and therefore this part of their provision comes under social services), or whether they are boarding for educational reasons. The preliminary findings from the Audit Commission's study into out-authority costs suggest that, even in England, where joint working is supposed to be more advanced in response to Every Child Matters, and where local education authorities have become part of children's services departments, the true costs of placements may not be known because separate budgets may still operate and the cost of all parts of the provision, including transport costs, is not necessarily totted up.

Successful strategies

- Having a clear vision of how the school needs to develop and being flexible about how to get there, so that opportunities can be seized as they arise

- Being prepared to adapt to changing and more complex needs, by adjusting the curriculum and the environment

- Working with mainstream partner schools to share staffing, resources and facilities

- Providing a resource on which a wide range of local authorities, schools and parents can draw

- Working closely with architects to make the most of any opportunity to improve the environment, keeping in mind the needs of the pupils who will be using the premises.

Points to ponder

- Does it make educational sense to offer a different curriculum to less able or more complex pupils?

- If so, should the same argument apply in mainstream schools?

Educating the severely and profoundly deaf

The second example is a school for the severely and profoundly deaf which offers some residential provision mainly because of distance. As explained in the first chapter, most conditions have their own continuum to describe a range from those who are slightly affected, to those who are very seriously affected. The loudness of sounds is measured in decibels and degrees of hearing loss are described in the following terms:

- Mild deafness: a loss of 20–40 decibels

- Moderate deafness: a loss of 41–70 decibels

- Severe deafness: 71–95 decibels

- Profound deafness: 95+ decibels

As there are not many children in any given area with this degree of hearing loss, such pupils will often have to travel some way to the nearest suitable provision. The school takes pupils whose statements say that they need sign language to access the curriculum. It employs a philosophy known as 'Total Communication', which includes British Sign Language. BSL was officially recognised as a language in its own right in 2003.

Total Communication

Total Communication is defined by the British Association of Teachers of the Deaf (BATOD) as follows:

Total Communication is an approach to language acquisition and mastery which uses a combination of oral, aural and manual components.

A debate that ran for centuries was over whether or not the deaf should be taught to speak. It was one of those frustrating arguments that almost entirely missed the point, for although it is obviously a huge advantage to learn to speak if at all possible, the main focus should have been on how to ensure that deaf children acquire language. Words have been described as *the tools of thought* and without language, those who are profoundly deaf, or, indeed, anyone who has difficulty acquiring language, is severely restricted in their ability to build up concepts, to understand the world around them and to be able to communicate their thoughts to others.

Mabel Davis, the head teacher, of the school in the next case study, describes her philosophy of Total Communication for teaching children who are deaf as follows:

> *It puts the child first. No two children will be the same, so teachers have to be able to draw on the right combination for each pupil when designing a teaching programme for them.*

At her school, this means using BSL, other signing systems, residual hearing, speech, lipreading and visual resources. As BSL does not have a written form, the school also uses other signing systems, such as Signed English, to help pupils' grammatical awareness. The school has a number of staff, including the head teacher, who are themselves deaf. The school's population includes a number of children whose deafness was caused by being born very prematurely.

Case study: Heathlands School for Deaf Children

Heathlands in Hertfordshire caters for 115 pupils aged 3–16 years who are severely or profoundly deaf. It has residential provision for 40 pupils. Although most board on a weekly basis and do so because of distance, a few from both deaf and hearing families may board for a time because of a difficult family situation, or because of the social benefits it can provide. Over 20 local authorities send children to the school.

The boarding provision is attached to the primary department, but with its own entrance, so that it is clearly demarcated from the school. Children who board are encouraged to play an active part in developing the provision they want. They help to plan the menus and they have helped to choose the decorations and furnishings for their rooms. They have worked together to create murals for the walls of their sitting rooms.

Since 1997, Heathlands has developed the unusual concept of *a school within a school* for its pupils of secondary age. Most attend Heathlands at Townsend, (Townsend being a mainstream secondary school in the same town), where Heathlands pupils have their own accommodation and staff, joining the other students for about 30 per cent of the curriculum. Those for whom the pace of a mainstream curriculum is inappropriate attend Heathlands at St Luke's, which is a special school for secondary pupils who have moderate learning difficulties (MLD).

Heathlands' development of schools within schools, means not only that pupils with a severe or profound hearing loss can receive the specialist help they need within a mainstream setting, but that they have the opportunity both to mix with hearing students and to have a peer group of the deaf as well. Signing classes are offered to the hearing pupils

▶

and have proved popular. At the primary level, an integration programme has been running in local schools for over twenty years and involves individuals, or groups of pupils, spending time in one of a number of local primary schools with which Heathlands has forged close links. Groups of pupils from mainstream classes also spend time at Heathlands to gain an understanding of sign language and how to relate to pupils who are deaf. (A poster that can be used to help the integration of pupils who are deaf is given on page 73.)

In line with Every Child Matters, pupils at Heathlands are increasingly encouraged to be involved in decision-making. Many assemblies are based on the five outcomes, when topics introduced are followed up in class and then brought back for further discussion and development. A school council has been formed for the primary pupils. (Its development is outlined on page 75, as a guide to others who want to establish a school council.)

In the same way that some believe every child has the right to be educated in a mainstream school, others, particularly some from the deaf community, have claimed that deaf children have a right to be educated with children who have similar needs. Farrell points out that:

Some deaf people are claiming a 'human right' to have deaf children educated together in a special school where they can communicate with one another because they are a linguistic minority. (Farrell, 2006: 20)

Mabel Davis' view is that pupils at her school get the best of both worlds: specialist teaching and resources that allow them to become fluent in both English and BSL, while having plenty of opportunities to be educated alongside their peers in mainstream schools. A pro forma developed by the school as an Individual Integration Plan for primary pupils follows on page 74 and may prove helpful to other schools integrating pupils with SEN, whether or not they are hearing impaired. It has proved helpful in ensuring that the purpose of the child being integrated is understood by both schools, and his or her progress can be measured against the targets and objectives agreed at the outset.

Successful strategies

- Making sure that opportunities for integration are carefully planned and that the schools involved are clear about the aims

- Introducing a school council and linking it with the school's PHSCE curriculum

- Giving pupils the maximum amount of specialist support at the primary stage, so that they have the skills to work alongside their mainstream peers for their secondary career

- Letting pupils know the outcomes of any suggestions they put forward, so they realise they can influence the way in which the school is run

- Avoiding too much of a top-down approach by handing over initiatives once they are launched and then keeping a check on progress.

How we can welcome and work with our deaf friends

'I make sure that my deaf friends are always included'

'I face my friends when talking'

'I wait until my friends are looking at me before I speak'

'I never stand with my back to the window when talking'

'My speech is clear and not too fast or too slow'

'I never cover my mouth while speaking'

'I write down words when needed'

'I never reply on behalf of my deaf friends but will pass on a message'

P Figure 4.1 Poster used at Heathlands School
Every Child Included, Paul Chapman Publishing © Rona Tutt, 2007

Termly Individual Plan

Name   Class   Date

Educational targets	Learning objectives this term	Provision

Review date..................

Progress

Figure 4.2 Individual Integration Plan used at Heathlands School
Every Child Included, Paul Chapman Publishing © Rona Tutt, 2007

Rationale for establishing a school council within the primary department

To provide an ideal opportunity for pupils to get more involved in the way the school is run.

It is the responsibility of the councillors to ensure they express both their own views and the views of the pupils they represent.

The school council will benefit the whole school, pupils and teachers. It will provide opportunities for pupils to develop and practise listening, communication and negotiation skills. It will also provide scope for exploring what being a good citizen means. It will provide an active learning experience that will be supported by a discrete and cross curricular PHSCE curriculum.

Time and venue for meetings

- Council to meet fortnightly
- During assembly on Tuesday/Wednesday for half an hour
- In the library

If pupils are committed to becoming councillors and taking an active role, they should not be penalised by missing break/lunchtimes for meetings.

Membership

- 2 teachers
- 2 elected representatives from each of Years 3–6
- Other interested staff

Budget

School council badges

Other expenses that occur

Introducing school councils to Key Stage 2 pupils

1   Why have a school council?

     How does a school council work?

     The role of a councillor

2   Becoming a councillor and the election process (secret ballots)

What next?

Election process can take place during PHSCE time in class on Friday following assembly.

First meeting held for:

- Team to get to know each other
- Set the agenda
- Introduce the focus 'Improving our playground'
- Find out how school council meetings are run

 Figure 4.3 School council at Heathlands School for the Deaf
Every Child Included, Paul Chapman Publishing © Rona Tutt, 2007

> ## Points to ponder
>
> ■ Should there be a continuing role for special schools catering for pupils who are deaf? If so, who should attend them? If not, what provision should be put in their place?
>
> ■ What are the best ways of breaking down the barriers between children who are deaf and those who can hear?

Audit of low incidence needs

In the wake of the government's SEN Strategy, *Removing Barriers to Achievement*, the DfES commissioned an audit of provision for 'low incidence needs.' Children who are described as having 'low incidence needs' are the most complex, and therefore the most costly, of those on the SEN continuum. Some of those who have low incidence needs will require boarding provision, because there will only be a few children with similar needs in any one area. This was the case with pupils at Heathlands (who would all be described as 'low incidence', because of the degree of their hearing loss), where children travel to the school from over twenty different local authorities. As Ysgol Plas Brondyffryn takes pupils from right across the autistic spectrum, some, but not all, will come within the definition of 'low incidence.' Again, serving a wide area as a regional resource, some needed boarding provision.

The case studies in the next section are examples of schools where the residential side has developed primarily in response to the needs of the pupils and their families rather than distance, although the nature of their needs is very different. In the case of one school, few of the pupils would be classified as having 'low incidence needs'; in the final example, all the pupils come under this category.

The focus of the audit was to:

- ■ Look at how local authorities were meeting the needs of children with low incidence SEN

- ■ Explore gaps in the provision currently available

- ■ Consider how this information could be used to assist regional and local planning

- ■ Make recommendations, including the development of 'Regional Centres of Expertise', so that, wherever the child lives, there would be access to a similar range of provision. (Case Study 9, Ysgol Plas Brondyffryn, which featured in the first case study in this chapter, is referred to as a Regional Centre for part of Wales, although Wales was not covered in audit.)

The research was carried out during 2005–06 by Peter Gray and his colleagues. Gray's Report, *National Audit of Support, Services and Provision for Children with Low Incidence Needs*, was published in 2006. The six categories of low incidence needs that were included by the DfES in the project specification for the audit were:

1 Multi-sensory impairments

2 Severe visual impairment

3 Severe/profound hearing impairment

4 Profound and multiple learning difficulties

5 Severe autistic spectrum disorders

6 Severe behavioural, emotional and social difficulties

However, once the research was underway, Gray and his team found it helpful to develop an operational definition. This was arrived at by thinking in terms of three overlapping circles, each one representing one of the following:

1 The rarity of the condition

2 The severity of the condition

3 Whether out of authority placement was likely to be needed

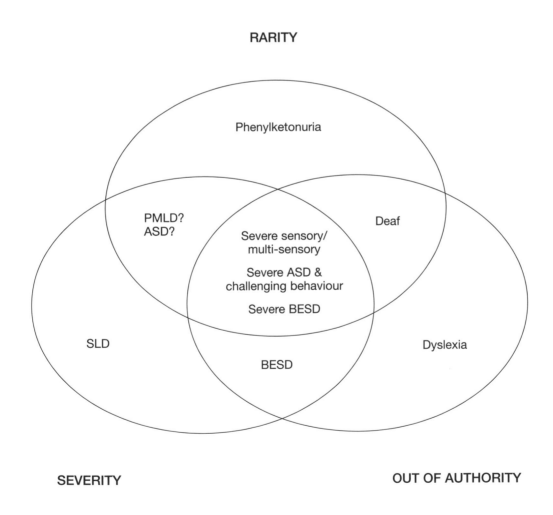

Figure 4.4 Towards an operational definition of 'low incidence needs' (DfES, 2006c)

This resulted in the following conditions being singled out as meeting the definition of low incidence needs:

- Severe sensory and multi-sensory difficulties (which combined 1, 2 and 3 of the specification)

- Severe ASD and challenging behaviour (number 5 in the specification)

- Severe BESD (number 6 in the specification)

Although these three categories were the ones Gray and his team concentrated on, they also recognised that profound and multiple learning difficulties (number 4 in the specification) is considered by many to be a low incidence condition. Another group labelled 'physical/health care needs', was also raised during the research for the audit. Some of the issues relating to these groups are included in the findings.

The word 'severe' is very significant in this context. Examples have already been given of a continuum of severity within the SEN continuum, showing that people with the same condition are affected to varying degrees. Gray and his colleagues concentrated on these conditions in their most severe form in order to ensure that they were focusing on low incidence needs, rather than the wider group of children who have the same difficulties, but to a lesser extent. Gray produced a series of recommendations for filling the gaps he discovered in the provision available and he also considered the idea of Regional Centres of Excellence, and how they might best be created. In the SEN Strategy, the aim of having these Regional Centres was said to be:

To achieve a more consistent coverage of specialist expertise across the country so that all schools know where to find the help they need. (DfES, 2004: paragraph 2.30)

In his recommendations, Gray made three suggestions for the development of Regional Centres of Excellence. The first of these was to link them with the specialist special schools programme that is already underway (see Chapter 1). The second suggestion was that each local authority would receive some money to develop either physical or 'virtual' centres to improve local capacity in a way that addressed the gaps revealed by the audit. His favoured option was one that would unite elements of the first and second approaches:

A third option would be to draw together the development of specialist special schools and other low incidence initiatives within a more coordinated strategic regional planning framework. (DfES, 2006c: paragraph 7.45)

Study by the Audit Commission

In addition to the work by Gray, the Audit Commission, which has produced many useful reports on SEN, also carried out a study in 2006. Although there was some overlap with Gray's work, the study had a narrower and more specific focus; it was concerned with the cost of out-authority placements in non-maintained and independent residential schools. The study looked at the way local authorities approached:

- Strategic planning

- Placement decisions

- Managing placements

- Managing budgets

As well as the National Audit this study too was concerned with low incidence needs, which the study defined as children who were being supported by specialist health and education services and many by social services as well. Preliminary findings suggest that there has not been an increase in the numbers attending out-authority placements, but that the costs of such placements have risen steeply. So far, the study has found that there was little joint planning across services and expressed the hope that the development of children's trusts (see Chapter 1) would help to push this forward.

Residential provision to meet needs

The second reason given at the beginning of this chapter for why schools have residential places was that it is sometimes the nature of the child's difficulties, their family circumstances or both, rather than distance, that is the main reason why they board. The two examples in this section illustrate the type of needs pupils have that may be addressed partly, or almost entirely, through residential provision.

Educating those with MLD and other complex needs

On the whole, the school in the next example is not used as out-authority provision, but to meet the needs of pupils and their families in an area of marked social deprivation. As previously pointed out, pupils with MLD are increasingly to be found in mainstream provision; a residential school for such pupils is even less common. Pupils who have moderate learning difficulties are the largest group under the SEN umbrella, yet schools specifically for them are diminishing in number. This may be because they are seen as the easiest pupils to integrate, in terms of not needing specialist equipment or resources, but simply needing to be given extra support in understanding new concepts, allowed more time to process information and given longer to produce their work. Local authorities have taken various approaches to the education of these children. Many are given extra help in mainstream classes. Some authorities have created units or bases attached to mainstream schools, where pupils can receive additional help for part of the school day. Some MLD schools have been merged with other types of special schools, such as those for pupils with severe learning difficulties (SLD) or behavioural, emotional and social difficulties (BESD). Others have kept their label as schools for pupils with MLD, but their populations have become more diverse.

The next case study illustrates this more diverse intake. Although still described as a school for children with MLD, about half the pupils have social, emotional and behavioural difficulties (BESD). Some of these pupils with BESD have MLD as well, while others will be working at a similar level to pupils with MLD, because their behavioural difficulties have impinged on, and inhibited, their ability to learn. Most of the pupils would fall outside Gray's definition of having low incidence needs, but it is the combination that some of them have of low level cognitive ability, marked behavioural difficulties and unsettled home circumstance, that indicate a residential placement may help their development. The school has good working links with the pupil referral unit (PRU) for Key Stage 1 pupils that shares its site. For instance, staff have worked together on trying out the Common Assessment Framework (CAF). David Field, the head teacher of the MLD school, has been involved in the delivery of CAF training, which is being introduced as part of Every Child Matters. Its purpose is to ensure that all three main services, (education, health and social care) use the same approach in the early stages of assessment.

The Common Assessment Framework (CAF)

The Common Assessment Framework has been extensively piloted and changes made as a result of the trials. It is already being used in some areas and is due to be fully in place by 2008. The CAF is a common assessment tool to be used by practitioners across the services, as a way of finding out which children have additional needs and what support they require in order to make progress against the five outcomes of ECM. Once it is in place it should help to make early intervention better organised across the services.

For its younger pupils, the school has developed the 'nurture group' model (as described in Chapter 2), so that all Key Stage 2 pupils are able to benefit from it. Now, a similar approach is being created for older pupils, some of whom have been out of school for some time and need a very gradual reintroduction to life in the classroom.

Case study: The Ashley School

The Ashley School in Suffolk caters for 125 pupils aged 7–16. Described as a school for pupils who have moderate learning difficulties, it caters for pupils who have complex learning, social or emotional needs, who have failed to make progress in mainstream schools and whose attainments are, in most cases, between P7 and level 3 of the National Curriculum. Although the majority live in the town where the school is situated, there are 30 places for boarders and a third of the school accesses this provision and/or the extended school day, which runs until 8 p.m on Mondays to Thursdays.

The extended day and flexible residential provision, where pupils can stay for two or four nights a week, eases the strain on some of the families in an area of social and economic deprivation. Likewise, for a number of children in care (as noted with the school in Wales), foster family arrangements are less likely to break down when the care of the children is split between the foster family and the school.

▶

The head teacher, David Field, has brought together the residential and educational aspects of the school by replacing a separate 'head of care' post with a pupil services manager, who is responsible for child protection issues and the welfare of 'looked after' children across the school, regardless of whether or not they happen to be in residence. The integration of the normal school day, the extended provision (which includes a variety of lunchtime clubs) and residential accommodation, offers a very wide range of activities and choice for pupils whose cognitive difficulties are compounded by behavioural, emotional and social difficulties.

The Ashley School has planned a nurture style environment for Key Stage 3 students who need to be enticed back into a school environment that they may have been away from for a number of months, or even years. The plan is to start them in a more informal, home-like environment on the school site, before expecting them to attend classes. Once they have grown used to being back in school and developed sufficient confidence, they will attend lessons with their peers.

The school has developed a particularly extensive range of courses for older students: a vocational and recreational studies course in conjunction with the adjacent high school and accredited courses run by a consortium of all the secondary schools and a college, which serves pupils who can benefit across the consortium of schools. (Details of these courses are on page 83, to provide a template that may be useful for other schools.)

The school's latest Ofsted report, describes some of the pupils 'having earlier damaging school care experiences', and 'fractured experiences in school' before moving to a special school. The school works closely alongside social care services to provide a supportive, stable environment. Systematic analysis of the school's data and comprehensive assessment procedures, has led to additional time, effort and resources being provided for children in care, so that their achievements are now in line with those of their peers at the school.

David Field has been developing charts linking the five outcomes of ECM to both the statutory curriculum and the other main areas of the school's work. This is given as a photocopiable resource on page 84, in case schools wish to use it as a model for their own versions. This could be a useful way of demonstrating how the five outcomes are being addressed through all aspects of the school's work. ('Flat 28' refers to the new provision for Key Stage 3 pupils who are being reintroduced into school life.) Like Baytree School in the previous chapter, The Ashley School hopes to become a specialist school in the SEN specialism of cognition and learning.

Successful strategies

- Integrating education and care by having key staff who work across both elements

- Providing a halfway house by having an extended day that can be used to give further opportunities to those who do not necessarily need to board, but who may not have similar opportunities available at their local schools

- Providing a range of activities in the lunch break in order to help pupils who find it hard to organise their free time

- Developing a vocational and recreational studies programme for Key Stage 4 students

- Analysing the progress of groups of pupils and putting extra resources into those who are particularly vulnerable or in care

---

Points to ponder

- Is there a role for schools that concentrate on educating pupils with MLD, or can they be equally well provided for in a mainstream environment?

- Is there a case to be made for special schools that provide for pupils with MLD who have additional difficulties, for example MLD/BESD, MLD/ASD, etc., where the combination of their difficulties may make it harder for them to thrive in a mainstream environment?

- Should the social needs of students and their families be taken into consideration when deciding on an appropriate placement?

The Ashley School

A curriculum for students with SEN at Key Stage 4

1 A Vocational and Recreational Studies Programme (VRS)

This has been developed over the last five years, in conjunction with the neighbouring high school, which is a Business and Enterprise College. This means that pupils with special needs at the high school also benefit from the programme, which draws on staff from the FE college and other trainers. The *vocational strand* is designed to improve students' chances of entering training or employment by giving them taster courses in a range of occupations, including: horticulture, carpentry, jewellery making, social care, as well as exploring opportunities for voluntary work.

The *recreational element* is designed to give students ideas for how to use their leisure time. It includes activities such as canoeing, orienteering, rock climbing and fishing, and trips to libraries, sports centres and youth clubs. Awards and qualifications that can be gained include:

- Duke of Edinburgh Award scheme

- St John Ambulance Young Life Savers Award

- Certificates in Food Hygiene and the Health and Safety in the Workplace, both from the Chartered Institute of Environmental Health

2 Other accredited courses

The school works in partnership with all the local high schools and the college to offer a range of accredited courses. Each of the local schools has a specialism: one is in sport and leisure, another in business studies and a third in ICT. The college adds catering and The Ashley School offers construction. This means that the consortium can provide between them the following pathways:

- Sport and leisure

- Retail

- Technical

- Catering

- Construction

Students in any of the schools in the consortium who will benefit, can participate in these courses.

Figure 4.5 Vocational and recreational studies programme at the Ashley School
Every Child Included, Paul Chapman Publishing © Rona Tutt, 2007

Area	English	Maths	Science	ICT	D+T	V.R.S.	PSHE	History and Geography	PE and Outdoor Education	Art and Music	Citizenship/ School Council	Beliefs and values/ assemblies
Achieve economic well-being												
Making a positive contribution												
Enjoying and achieving												
Be healthy												
Staying safe												

P Figure 4.6 Mapping provision to address the ECM outcomes: The Taught Curriculum
Every Child Included, Paul Chapman Publishing © Rona Tutt, 2007

Area	Residence and extended day provision	Administration	Pupil support worker	Flat 28 Project	Nurture provision at KS2	Duke of Edinburgh Award scheme	School visits
Achieve economic well-being							
Making a positive contribution							
Enjoying and achieving							
Be healthy							
Staying safe							

Figure 4.7 Mapping provision to address the ECM outcomes *The Extended Curriculum*

Every Child Included, Paul Chapman Publishing © Rona Tutt, 2007

Educating those with the most complex needs

The final case study in this chapter is a second school that provides residential facilities because of the nature of the children's needs, rather than primarily because of distance. It caters for pupils whose needs are sufficiently severe for almost all of them to have placements all year round. This is an independent residential school in the West Midlands run by a registered charity as a not-for-profit organisation. It enjoys the freedom to innovate that its independent status provides. All the students, like those at Heathlands, are those with low incidence needs.

Over the last decade, an increasing number of pupils on the autistic spectrum have joined the community, so that they now represent over half the school's population. However, the specific way in which they are taught, using the very structured and visual approach of the TEACCH method (Treatment and Education of Autistic and related Communication Handicapped Children), and the fact that many have severe learning difficulties in addition to their autism, means that the approach to teaching them is also applicable to pupils with very limited cognitive capacity who do not have a diagnosis of autism.

According to research done by Jordan et al. (1998), for what was then the Department for Education and Employment, TEACCH is the most commonly employed method for educating children on the autistic spectrum:

> *Many of the specialist schools and units in the UK have adopted some TEACCH ideas and of the major approaches, this is the one most likely to be evident within UK schools and units, both mainstream and special. (Jordan et al., 1998: 81)*

The TEACCH Aproach

Designed by Mesibov, Schopler and colleagues at the University of North Carolina over 30 years ago, TEACCH adapts the environment to accommodate the needs of those with ASD. Typically, each student has his or her own workstation and an individual timetable, in pictures, signs or words. Short tasks are presented in the form of carefully graded activities within a clear routine, and there is a well-defined beginning and end to each session. There is a strong emphasis on visually presented material, as people with ASD often have visual strengths, rather than learning easily through language.

Case study: Sunfield School

Sunfield is a DfES registered Independent Residential Special School, and, under the Care Standards Act 2002, it is also registered as a children's home. It caters for children and young people aged 6–19, whose needs are so severe and complex, that over 70 of the 80 places available are for children and young people who need to be in residence throughout the year. Places are paid for by local authorities and over 40 different ones have funded children to attend. As well as the newer population of children with ASD, the school has

▶

found that the nature of the difficulties of the other children has changed over time, due, in part to premature babies surviving at a much earlier stage of their development.

As well as the school, which is being rebuilt to meet the needs of the changing population, there are twelve residential houses and two family centres, where families can stay in self-contained accommodation. The extensive site provides plenty of scope for play, the outdoor curriculum and, for the older students, work experience in animal management and horticulture.

The principal is very clear that his aim is to provide a complementary service to that which neighbouring local authorities are able to provide. He believes that the most significant aspect of Sunfield's work is its ability to be family-centred. He says:

We do not take in children; we welcome families as part of our community. After all, every adult matters as well.

Siblings are also supported through a very active Siblings Group, in recognition of the fact that brothers and sisters of disabled children can feel very left out.

Since Barry Carpenter, took over in 1997, Sunfield has developed:

■ A link with 'Division TEACCH' at the University of North Carolina, through which Sunfield has become a centre for delivering training in the TEACCH approach. It is also part of the University of Worcester, delivering an in-house foundation degree in learning support

■ An Assessment and Outreach Centre to support mainstream and special schools, families, social services and other agencies, in the education and care of children and young people with challenging behaviour and ASD

■ A Research Institute and a Professional Development Centre that puts on courses and conferences for parents and a wide range of professionals.

In the entrance hall at Sunfield, there are five display boards showing how each of the ECM outcomes are being implemented. The school's aims are also on display, having been reviewed regularly with staff, parents and governors. The Senior Leadership team has cross-referenced the school's aims and the five outcomes with the requirements of Ofsted and CSCI (Commission for Social Care Inspection). This is provided as a blueprint that others with residential provision may care to adapt (see page 88).

When the school was established in the 1930s, it was at a time when those with significant learning difficulties were kept out of the public gaze. Now, the school bases its work on supporting the whole family and provides a resource that has an influence far beyond its boundaries.

Table 4.1: Sunfield framework for integrated quality assurance

Sunfield aim \ ECM outcomes	Being healthy	Staying safe	Enjoying and achieving	Making a positive contribution	Achieving economic well-being	Management
1. To live as independently as possible	*Section 162a Welfare, health and safety of pupils* The school shall draw up and implement a written policy to prevent bullying, safeguard and promote the welfare of students, safeguard and promote the H&S of students on activities out of school and promote the good behaviour of students and set out the policy on rewards and sanctions *Suitability of proprietors and staff* The requirements for the accommodation as set out in regulation 5 a–u are met fully. Students have opportunities to plan, shop for and prepare meals NMSCH10. Students exercise choice in selecting options in the main dining room and houses NMSCH. Children live in a healthy environment and their health needs are identified and services are provided to meet them, and their good health is promoted NMSCH12.	*Section 162a Welfare, health and safety of pupils* The school shall draw up and implement a written policy to prevent bullying, safeguard and promote the welfare of students, safeguard and promote the H&S of students on activities out of school and promote the good behaviour of students and set out the policy on rewards and sanctions. Homes provide physical safety and security NMSCH26. *Section 162a suitability of proprietors and staff* All require CRB and identity checks are carried out. The requirements for the accommodation as set out in regulation 5 a–u are met fully.	*Student academic and life skills achievement* Students receive individual support when they need it NMSCH7. *Section 162a Quality of education provided* The school will have a written policy on the curriculum, supported by appropriate plans and SoW, which provides for: See Regulations 2003 Schedule 1 (2) a–i Teaching in the school will: See Regulations 2003 Schedule 1(3) a–h	*Section 162a SMSC development of pupils* The school will promote principles which enable students to develop self-knowledge, self-esteem and self-confidence; enable them to tell right from wrong; encourage them to accept responsibility for their behaviour, show initiative and understand how they can contribute to the community; provide students with a broad knowledge of institutions and services in England and assist them to respect and appreciate their own and others' cultures. Students are encouraged and supported to make decisions about their lives and to influence the way in which the home is run. No student is assumed to be unable to communicate their views NMSCH8. Students enjoy sound relationships with staff based on honesty and mutual respect NMSCH21.	Transition arrangments for students' admission to, movement through and exit from the school are effective NMSCH5. Students receive care which helps to prepare them and support them into adulthood NMSCH6. Students are encouraged and enabled to choose their own clothes and personal requisites and have these needs met fully NMSCH11. Students' privacy is respected when washing NMSCH25.	Children receive the care and services they need from competent staff NMSCH29. Children enjoy the stability of efficiently run homes NMSCH34. Children's needs, development and progress are recorded to reflect their individuality NMSCH35. *Section 162a suitability of proprietors and staff* The requirements for the accommodation as set out in regulation 5 a–u are met fully.

P Table 4.1: Sunfield framework for integrated quality assurance

Every Child Included Paul Chapman Publishing © Rona Tutt 2007

Student Mission Statement

Sunfield   **wants**   **everyone**   **to find out**   **what**   **they**   **can do.** **Sunfield**

wants   **everyone**   **to**   **know**   **life**   **is**   **good.**

At   **Sunfield,**   **we**   **respect** **everybody**   **and**   **say**   **that**   **everybody**   **is**

special.

We   **want**   **to show** **everyone**   **at**   **Sunfield**   **how**   **to learn,**

understand   **and**   **be**   **happy.**

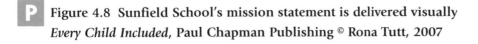

Figure 4.8 Sunfield School's mission statement is delivered visually
Every Child Included, Paul Chapman Publishing © Rona Tutt, 2007

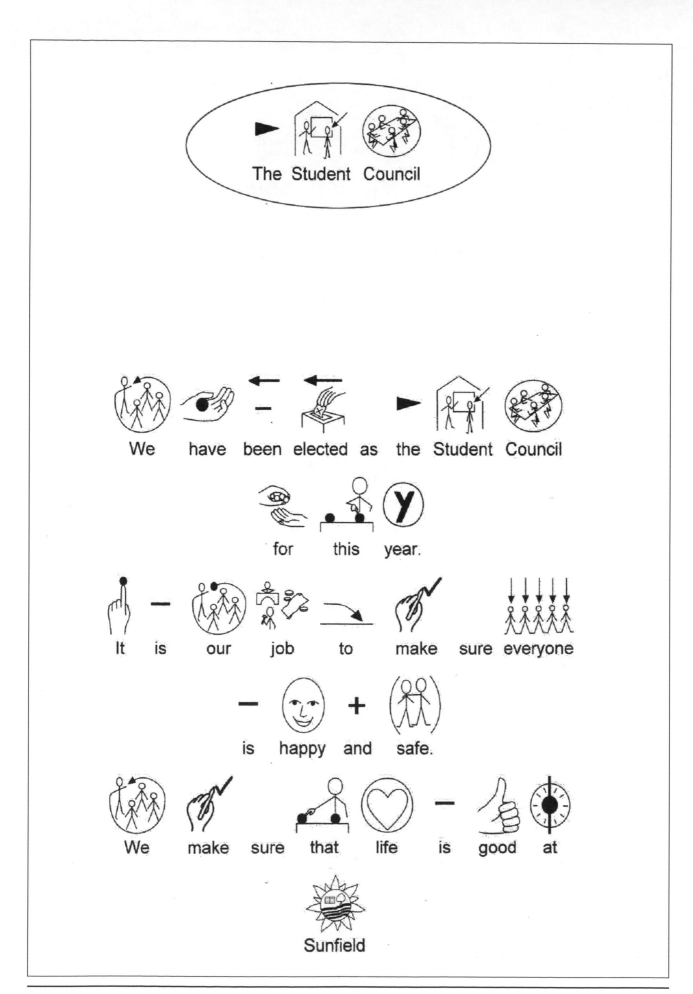

Figure 4.9 Sunfield School's student council message is also delivered visually
Every Child Included, Paul Chapman Publishing © Rona Tutt, 2007

Successful strategies

- Having on display how the school is embedding the five outcomes in its practice, illustrated through pictures, photographs and words

- Discussing annually with staff, students, parents and governors, the school's aims and having them publicly displayed

- Having in place mechanisms to ensure that all staff work together to record progress towards targets and that pupils and parents are fully involved

- Having clear policies and procedures that all staff agree and follow

- Giving a high profile to the professional development of all staff, so that they acquire the skills they need to deal with an increasingly complex population

---

Points to ponder

- How have society's attitudes changed to people who are 'different'?

- Does 52-week provision enable those with the most complex and severe needs to feel more included in community life than would otherwise be the case?

- Are there any other ways this might be achieved?

Addressing inclusion in residential special schools

Residential schools are no different from other schools in having to adapt to more complex populations. More places for children and young people requiring 52 weekly placements are seen as necessary, for instance, as a result of a growing number of children with ASD who also have very challenging behaviour, or because babies are surviving after being born at an increasingly premature stage. However severe the needs of the pupils are already, the schools are prepared to adapt what they offer in order to meet the needs of even more complex pupils.

Another change affecting schools with residential provision would seem to be the support they can give to an increasing number of families, where a lack of stability combined with a measure of deprivation, makes it harder for them to cope with a child who demands a considerable degree of extra care and attention. Having the pressure taken off, even if only for part of the week, can help to keep families together. 'Looked after' children also may be easier to place with a family, if the care of that child is shared with the school. This should not be seen as benefiting the family rather than the child. A particular contribution special schools can make, and for those in difficult circumstances, schools with residential provision, is the stability and security of the comparatively small environment that they provide, where children are known to everyone and the numbers and staffing ratios make it easier to support both pupils and their families.

It might be expected that these schools would be less outward looking than other schools, functioning more as communities on their own, but this is far from the case. Even where a school was virtually entirely a boarding school, and provided for children all year round, there was no sense of isolation, but rather of a school having an impact far beyond its boundaries, and keen to use the experience built up over many years to inform and support others. The children themselves are being taken out regularly to broaden their experience and to provide them with a wide range of activities and opportunities.

Links with mainstream schools are being built up in a number of different ways. In one school, this was through the opportunities brought about by the co-location of both its primary and secondary departments. In another, it was through creating a school within a school, in order to give its students with low incidence needs the best of both worlds. A third school was fully integrated with all the local secondary schools, so that between them, they were catering for students with SEN regardless of which school they attended. Just from this small sample, it is clear the progress that is being made in schools moving closer together and sharing responsibility for the pupils they educate. Much of this progress towards closer working has come about in the last few years and shows the determination of school leaders to move their schools forward and to seize new opportunities for growth.

Addressing Every Child Matters in residential special schools

Special schools with residential accommodation have particularly strong links across the services. Many of their pupils will have medical conditions that need close monitoring. Health professionals may undertake part of their training at a special school, including residential special schools. A range of therapists will be employed to work alongside teaching staff to support children's development. Social services will be involved with many of the children and families at the schools, particularly with children 'at risk' or those in care. Some schools employ their own social worker, or, if not, they will have someone on the staff who is responsible for maintaining those important links with social care.

In a way, special schools which have residential provision, may find it easier to provide an extended day than day special schools, as the school is already open all the time, and the schools have been used to providing a range of activities to keep boarders occupied beyond the school day. Indeed, the few schools that have 52 weekly placements could be seen as being as extended as it is possible to be in terms of the amount of time the school is open. One of the examples in this chapter was of a school that had made an extended day a key part of what it provides, so that pupils, whether boarders or not, can take part in a range of activities up until 8 p.m., giving them something positive to do in their free time and, again, being a way of relieving pressure on families.

Even in schools where pupils are most limited in their ability to communicate, ways are being found of listening to the children and obtaining their views. Signs and symbols can be used to help children put their views across and to help them understand the views of others. School councils are springing up to provide a forum for children's views, sometimes as part of the PSHCE curriculum (personal, social, health and citizenship education). More people, including governors and agencies specialising in listening to the views of children and young people, are dropping in unannounced in order to give pupils the opportunity to speak to someone beyond the school staff. This is particularly important in a residential situation, and even more so for pupils who have difficulty in expressing their views.

Points to remember

Residential placements enable pupils to: attend a school offering an appropriate education that would otherwise be out of reach and to have a 24-hour curriculum and a stable environment. These schools are as enterprising and outward-looking as any other type of provision in:

■ Adjusting to changing populations

■ Adapting to new expectations, including a dual role for special schools

■ Implementing Every Child Matters

Whether or not they are physically near mainstream provision, they have found ways of making meaningful links across the sectors, to provide richer experiences for their pupils and to share their skills and experience with others.

With an increased number of children displaying very complex needs, the demand for schools that can offer boarding is likely to continue, with such schools forming a vital part of the provision for SEN, not least for those with the most severe and/or low incidence needs

The five outcomes of ECM are being taken very seriously and schools are finding different ways of keeping these at the forefront of everyone's thinking, whether having them and how they are being implemented on public display, designing themes for assemblies around them, or finding ways of mapping them against all areas of the school's work, including the requirements of Ofsted and CSCI. It is perhaps surprising, and certainly inspiring, to find how schools working with pupils who have some of the most complex and severe needs are seeking new ways of moving forward. Whether looking at mainstream schools, or the whole range of special schools, those working with children and young people with SEN, are looking all the time for new ways of developing what they do to help their pupils overcome barriers to learning. Increasingly, they are working in partnership with each other to find the best ways of making sure all children feel included, are able to enjoy their school days and achieve their potential. The more limited that potential, the more important it is that it is maximised. All the time, schools are finding ways of bringing out the best in pupils with SEN, including those with the most significant and complex difficulties.

TEN TIPS FOR BEST PRACTICE

1 Grow your own staff

2 Integrate the work of teaching and care staff

3 Make everyone aware that they matter and have a vital part to play

4 Clarify roles and responsibilities

5 Ensure people feel they are part of a team

6 Foster a team spirit through constant communication

▶

7 Think in terms of working with families, including siblings, rather than individuals

8 Value the contribution of other professionals and develop a common language

9 Develop data that tells you which individuals and groups need targeting

10 Engender a sense of purpose, confidence and optimism in colleagues and pupils alike

Final thoughts

■ Think back to your ideas at the beginning of the chapter. Have you changed your views on boarding education and who may benefit from it?

■ If so, in what ways?

■ If not, how would you counteract the arguments that have been put forward in favour of boarding education for those with low incidence needs and/or suffering from a disrupted family lifestyle?

 # Recommended reading

Audit commission (2006) *The Cost of Out-authority Placements.*

Department for Education and Skills (2006) *National Audit of Support, Services and Provision for Children with Low Incidence Needs.* Research Report 729, Nottingham, DfES Publications

Jordan, R. *et al* (1998) *Educational Interventions for Children with Autism: A Literature Review of Recent and Current Research.* London: DfEE

CHAPTER 5

Pupil referral units, outreach, advisory and support services

This chapter outlines some of the support that is available to schools, in finding ways of making the curriculum accessible to pupils who have a variety of special educational needs. The following types of provision are identified:

■ Outreach work and services from special schools

■ Pupil referral units (PRUs)

■ Devolved services

■ Centrally retained services

Although the services are discussed under these four headings, the examples show that there are many connections between them.

The range of services available to schools

In the same way that it would be impossible to give an overview of developments across all types of mainstream and special schools, it is only possible to touch on some of the ways that support to schools is changing, in terms of who is delivering it and how it is being provided. At one time, local authorities were responsible for delivering most of the services schools needed to support them in their role, including the education of pupils with special educational needs. Now, although pupils with SEN remain one of the responsibilities of local authorities, services may be commissioned by them, rather than delivered directly. For instance, the increasing emphasis on a dual role for special schools has seen a growth in the number of outreach services from these schools, as one way of delivering support. Pupil referral units (PRUs) are now managed in a number of different ways. However they are managed, they support schools by being a source of alternative provision, and may themselves undertake outreach work. As part of the move to devolve more money to schools, local authorities have retained fewer services centrally. Examples of all these different ways of providing services to schools to support them in the education of pupils with SEN, are discussed in this chapter, including the role of both devolved and centrally funded services.

The background to changes in service delivery

In 1988, the Education Reform Act (ERA) brought in a raft of changes, including the National Curriculum, Ofsted inspections and Local Management of Schools (LMS). The delegation of budgets under LMS removed most of the budgeting and management aspects of schools from local authority control and the effects were far-reaching. One of the consequences of schools handling their own budgets was that local education authorities (LEAs as they were then), that had very large services found them harder to maintain, while the services that went out to delegation in the early days found it difficult to adjust to a totally new situation where they had to remain viable by charging schools. As schools had a degree of freedom over how they chose to spend their money, many sevices did not survive, or carried on in a much reduced form. At that time, the future for support services looked very uncertain.

In 2000, the DfEE (as it was then) published *The Role of the Local Education Authority*, which explained the role of the LEA in the following terms:

> *We believe that education authorities have precise and limited functions. It is not their role to run or intervene in schools, except those which are in danger of, or have fallen into, special measures or serious weaknesses: nor should they seek to provide directly all education services in their areas. Rather their job is to provide certain specific planning and support functions which are essential to guarantee adequate school provision. (DfEE, 2000: paragraph 4)*

So a more open market for school services was encouraged, with schools deciding which one offered best value and was the most cost effective provider from a range of public, private and voluntary sector organisations. Within this changing context for local education authorities however, SEN provision remained one of the duties that LEAs could not pass on to individual schools, so LEAs were expected to continue to run:

> *high quality education psychology and support teaching services, linking with social and health services and planning – often across authorities – the use of scarce resources so that individual children can benefit from coordinated provision through their school. (DfEE, 2000: paragraph 13a)*

The *Report of the Special Schools Working Group* (2003), gave an overview of how specialist support and advice to schools was being delivered:

> *Local authorities have historically played an important role in providing this through the educational psychology service, behaviour support teams, and teams of specialist teachers. The ways of providing support vary. Some local authorities have large central teams, many have delegated resources enabling schools to 'buy back' support, and some fund outreach services provided by special schools and voluntary sector organisations. (DfES, 2003: paragraph 2.34)*

The Children Act (2004) underlined this move to make local authorities, in their new form as Children's Services, *commissioners* of services, including drawing on the expertise of the private and voluntary sectors, with services transforming themselves into centres of expertise to advise and support schools in making provision. At the same time, there was also a growing realisation, both locally and nationally, that support services represented a valuable educational asset. Some services have built on this to develop their expertise to cover particular aspects, such as low incidence needs, ASD and severe dyslexia/dyspraxia.

In its *Response to the Education and Skills Committee Report on Special Educational Needs* (2006) the government wrote that:

Services may be centrally run, provided by special schools on outreach or through mainstream schools working in partnership with Pupil Referral Units and special schools. But the government is clear that such services must be provided if we are to increase access for staff to specialist advice and support. (paragraph 33)

This sums up how services have moved from being provided largely by local authorities to a situation where there are many providers. A further source of support may, in future, be delivered through the Regional Centres of Expertise (RCEs) mentioned in the last chapter. Pump priming is available for 2006–07 and again for 2007–08 for these to be established, in collaboration with the Regional Partnerships (formerly known as the SEN Regional Partnerships).

Questions for reflection

■ Do you think it has been helpful for schools to decide which services to buy in?

■ Do you see any dangers in schools and governing bodies making the decisions?

■ Do you know what services are available in your area and does the system for providing them work well or not?

Services run by special schools

As mentioned in previous chapters, the government's SEN Strategy, *Removing Barriers to Achievement* (2004), clarified that special schools should have a dual role: educating some of the pupils with the most complex needs and working closely with local schools to support them in their work with pupils who have SEN. In October 2005, the DfES launched a consultation paper entitled, *Draft Standards for SEN Support and Outreach Services*, which brings together common standards for SEN Advisory and Support Services, including outreach services from both special and mainstream schools. It is the first time that standards for these services have been laid down. Taking into consideration some of the work that had been done in this area, the DfES (2005b) suggested the following four headings:

1 The service to have a clear purpose which takes into account other provision in the area and the needs of particular schools and pupils

2 The service has experienced, well-qualified staff to deliver a high quality service

3 Services are led and managed to promote change in schools

4 Pupils and parents are fully involved in the development of services

While the outcome of this consultation is still awaited, the need to have quality assurance, as services multiply and diversify, is very clear. The title of the consultation paper reflects that of an Ofsted report in 2005, *Inclusion: The Impact of LEA Support and Outreach Services*, which also brought together support services and outreach, indicating a rise in the status of outreach, from a service that has been delivered for many years mainly on an ad hoc basis, to being seen as an integral part of the continuum of support to be offered to schools.

While some special schools are just beginning outreach work, others have run outreach services for a considerable time. The Ofsted report, *Inclusion: Does it Matter Where Pupils are Taught* (2006) said that:

> *Special schools should collaborate and share expertise more effectively to develop specialist teaching in mainstream schools, with the support of the LA and in line with other services. (Ofsted, 2006: 5)*

It is this need to coordinate the work of special schools and other services available in the local authority that is sometimes left to chance, rather than planned as a cohesive service, within which all the support available to schools is delivered in a coordinated manner. As the number and variety of services grows, it becomes even more essential that they complement each other rather than overlap. There is plenty of work that needs to be done in supporting schools, but it needs to be integrated within a strategic plan. The 2006 Ofsted report goes on to say that:

> *Special schools had a particular strength in carefully matching the skills and interests of staff to the needs of groups of pupils. But teachers in mainstream schools had better knowledge of individual subjects in the National Curriculum. (Ofsted, 2006: 10)*

The final sentence above is a useful reminder that when schools share expertise, it is of benefit to both sides. It is not as one dimensional as special schools doing a favour to mainstream schools by delivering outreach, but rather of that close collaboration being of mutual benefit. It is also the case that mainstream schools themselves are building up enough expertise in certain fields of SEN, to be able to provide support to colleagues. An example of a group of resourced primary schools working in this way is given later in this chapter (see page 101).

An example of two schools that were providing outreach services to the schools in their area long before it became as recognised as it is today are two schools in Hertfordshire. Colnbrook School, in the south of the county, and Woolgrove School in the north, are primary schools for pupils with moderate learning difficulties (MLD). They have been delivering outreach since the early 1980s. Since 1996, they have also developed provision for pupils with autistic spectrum disorders (ASD) and this has become another aspect of their work in local schools. The outreach services grew in response to local need and were supported by the local authority. All teachers undertaking outreach work continue to be practising teachers in the schools, and have to complete successfully the authority's training for teachers involved in this type of work.

Outreach Services from two schools for pupils with MLD

For more than 20 years, and in response to local demand, Colnbrook and Woolgrove's Outreach Services have developed to include the following elements:

■ Working alongside mainstream colleagues in assessing pupils who are experiencing difficulties, and providing strategies and resources to support them

■ Managing a special needs resource centre open to all local schools, with materials available on loan, and information on various disorders and conditions

■ Using the whole school as a resource that staff can visit to observe in classrooms and to talk to teachers

■ Organising courses and training sessions for teachers and teaching assistants, many as 'twilight sessions' after school

■ Planning the transition of pupils into the special schools and reintegration programmes for those who are ready to return to mainstream education

A remark that is often made to outreach teachers is that their support on practical classroom strategies are particularly helpful, because they come from teachers who continue to be practitioners.

It became apparent from the case studies in the last two chapters, that special schools are reaching out to support mainstream colleagues in a number of different ways. The next example is of one of the special schools in Belfast, that was mentioned in Chapter 3, Harberton School. The school has developed a whole range of services to local schools, with the support of the Library Board (the equivalent in Northern Ireland of a local authority).

Services run by a special school in Belfast

As well as being a special school for pupils with MLD and other conditions, Harberton has developed the following services to local schools:

■ A diagnostic nursery for 8 pupils, to determine their need for mainstream, MLD or SLD placement

■ A nursery support service to support approximately 20 three-year-olds at a time, who are having difficulties settling in to mainstream nurseries

■ An outreach behaviour service to support up to 90 Key Stage 1 pupils who have been assessed as having BESD

■ An outreach learning service to support nearly 300 pupils in maintaining their places in mainstream schools

■ Units for children with reading difficulties that provide intensive support to pupils who have been diagnosed as dyslexic, including 13 full-time and 21 part-time pupils

Turning from Northern Ireland to Wales, an unusual facility has been developed by another special school that was also mentioned in Chapter 3. St Christopher's runs an Eco Centre, which is available to its own pupils, as well as to local primary and secondary schools. It is mentioned here because it also serves as an alternative form of provision for some of its own students from the school's behaviour support department, and for some students from local schools who are disaffected or not responding to the curriculum on offer, as well as for a few from the local pupil referral unit (PRU). Although not exclusively used by pupils with SEN, it has a particular role in providing a curriculum for those students whose behaviour is difficult to manage in a classroom environment, but who are responsive to an outdoor-based curriculum. This provides an active, practical approach to learning, and for some of the students, it has the added incentive that they can earn some money by learning how to grow and sell plants.

A special school's Eco Centre in Wales

St Christopher's Millennium Eco Centre is in an existing quarry on the edge of the town and its work is supported by Tarmac, which owns the quarry. It is run by the school to interest pupils in the environment. The main theme of the Eco Centre is sustainability: sustainable waste management and a sustainable lifestyle, which is promoted through an appreciation of the environment and how to live off the land. Pupils have been involved in the project from the start and have helped to create an unusually varied, creative and productive Eco Centre. On site, there is a classroom and a café, serving hot and cold drinks, as well as snacks. The site is used by local schools and other people for the following reasons:

- As part of a business enterprise, including growing and selling plants

- For work experience and access to accredited environmental courses

- To learn about the mechanics of quarrying, recycling, tree-planting, fence-building, bricklaying, maintaining allotments and willow weaving

- To take part in environmental projects

About 40 people a day use the site, including adults with learning difficulties, as well as individuals and groups from local primary and secondary schools.

Points to ponder

- Do you think it is a good idea for special schools to run outreach services?

- Should they run other services as well?

- If so, which ones do you think are most helpful to schools?

Pupil referral units (PRUs)

Pupil referral units were set up under the 1996 Education Act to make provision for pupils who are out of school for reasons such as exclusion or illness. Pupils can be dually registered at a PRU and at a school. A PRU may be for one of the key stage age groups, for primary or secondary pupils, or cover the whole of the age range. The majority of PRUs concentrate on those who have been excluded or who are at risk of exclusion. PRUs are officially both schools and 'education otherwise than at school'. There are differences from other schools in the way they are run. They have:

- A management committee rather than a governing body, and this committee may manage more than one PRU

- Pupils who can be dually registered at the PRU and at a local school

- No requirement to cover the National Curriculum in its entirety

- Different requirements from schools as regards the premises

Although not all the pupils at a PRU will necessarily have SEN, many will have recognised behavioural, emotional and social difficulties (BESD), for which some will be statemented. There are concerns that the pressures caused by the curriculum in its current form and the degree and style of testing that goes with it, result in some pupils reacting adversely to the demands made on them. Because they find it hard to cope, or are unmotivated by what is on offer, they respond by exhibiting nonchalant, defiant or aggressive behaviour. The conflict between the standards agenda, with its pressure on schools and their pupils to perform to certain standards, and the inclusion agenda, is apparent to all, except perhaps the politicians.

Some PRUs are managed by the head teacher of a special school. Cuckmere House, a BESD school in East Sussex, has a PRU for primary aged pupils within the special school, and oversees two other PRUs for older students elsewhere in the county. The New Rush Hall Group in Redbridge is an organisation that works with children who have BESD in various locations. It is one of the first schools to be designated a special school with a BESD specialism. It manages a range of services in conjunction with the local authority.

The New Rush Hall Group

The New Rush Hall Group works across a range of settings with youngsters who are experiencing social, emotional and behavioural difficulties. The group is made up of:

- **New Rush Hall School** which opened in 1991 and takes 72 pupils aged 5–16 who have BESD. The vast majority are boys. Several pupils have a diagnosis of AD/HD or ASD, including Asperger's syndrome. Some primary pupils are admitted on a part-time basis

- The school's **behaviour support outreach service** offers support both to mainstream schools and to individual students, offering both curriculum and counselling support

- **A Key Stage 3 PRU** is on another site for 16 Years 7–9 students, who have been, or are on the verge of being, excluded

- A **Key Stage 4 PRU** is on two separate sites: a college site and a factory unit for vocational based work

- **A Tuition Service** which is an all-age PRU, working with those who are temporarily out of school

- **An adolescent psychiatric unit** with residential, day and outpatient assessment for up to 35 teenagers is also available and on-site education

The head teacher, John d'Abbro, manages the group, with the school governors and local authority overseeing the resources and services.

As part of the move to find fresh ways of tackling behaviour, and particularly reducing exclusions, from January 2006 all secondary schools have been expected to form behaviour partnerships. Some schools have already been working together in this way for some time. The Chesil Education Partnership (also known as the Chesil Federation) in Dorset, for instance, is a collaborative of 28 schools: 4 secondaries, 14 primaries, 3 juniors, 3 infants, 2 special schools 1 PRU, and an FE college, which has been in operation since January 2004. One of its aims is for greater inclusion within its schools, including an aspiration to reduce permanent exclusions to zero. In September 2005, the Compass Centre was opened by the partnership to provide a range of alternative provision for pupils at Key Stages 1–4, with resources provided through partnership with the local authority.

The Compass Centre

The Compass is one of the larger PRUs. It caters for 111 pupils aged 4–16. Although a minority of students are school phobics or have already been excluded, the majority are either at risk of exclusion or have medical conditions. Most remain on the roll of their local school. The majority of the students are of secondary age. The Centre has existed under a different name since September 2005.

The Centre has one main base, but uses 14 other sites to provide a wide range of individualised learning opportunities. The pupils comment that they enjoy being in a place where their views are heard, they have a high level of individual attention and a greater degree of choice about the contents of the curriculum. They talk about the Centre being a more relaxed and less stressful environment than that of their previous placements. Although most of the students are low attainers when they arrive, records of what leavers have achieved indicate that the Centre has had a positive impact on their lives. Passes at GCSE, work-related learning and work experience placements stand them in good stead for the future.

Points to ponder

- What do you see as the value of PRUs?

- Which pupils do you think benefit the most from attending this type of provision?

- Does your school or service have any connection with the PRU in your area? If not, would it be useful to form any links?

Devolved services

As mentioned at the beginning of this chapter, since the local management of schools came about as a result of the 1988 Education Act, there has been growing pressure on local authorities to delegate an increasing share of their budget to schools. This has been given even greater emphasis by more recent legislation and documentation, including the government's *Choice for Parents, the Best Start for Children: Ten-Year Childcare Strategy* (Treasury, 2004) the White Paper *Higher Standards, Better Schools for All* (DfES, 2005c) and the subsequent *Education and Inspections Act* (DfES, 2006d), the *Youth Matters* (DfES, 2005d) and the Children Act of 2004. All of these describe a shift from local authorities being providers of services to commissioning services from other providers. One of the services that was at the forefront of the move to delegation was the North Lincolnshire SEN Support Service. Under its head teacher at the time, Tricia Barthorpe, it was one of the first services to become completely devolved, with all monies delegated to schools, and which succeeded in flourishing in an open market.

North Lincolnshire SEN Support Service (SENSS)

The service was established in 1996 as part of the new unitary authority to support pupils with SEN throughout Key Stages 1–4 and to provide for 150 Key Stage 3 and Key Stage 4 students at risk of permanent exclusion. All secondary schools in the town agreed to buy in to the service which made it viable, and with its position on the edge of a business park, SENSS was able to offer a wide range of opportunities to students who would otherwise have been in danger of having very little to show for their years in school. As well as improving their basic skills, a personalised curriculum was offered to each student to retain their interest and keep them motivated.

Having been at the forefront of the move to succeed in a climate of devolved funding, in 2006, North Lincolnshire Local Authority and SENSS pioneered *Procuring Services 2006–09*, giving private contractors the ability to tender under strict performance indicators, by which schools can judge which services are likely to be value for money.

Since 2004, as part of the North Lincolnshire policy, permanent exclusions have been reduced to nil at all key stages. In 2006, all Key Stage 4 students gained GCSEs, many at A to C grades, as well as a range of other qualifications.

Primary Support Bases (PSBs)

Another approach to avoiding exclusions at an early stage, while coordinating support for the county's pupils with behavioural and emotional difficulties in general, came about in Hertfordshire through developing an extended role for its 9 primary schools with BESD Units, now renamed Primary Support Bases (PSBs). This was done in the context of the authority's Behaviour and Achievement Strategy and in consultation with the PRUs, the BESD schools and the authority's Behaviour Support Team, which has a similar role to the national Behaviour and Education Support Teams (BESTs). In Hertfordshire, the funding for the PSBs is delegated to the resourced schools budgets and identified separately within their budget shares.

Behaviour and Education Support Teams (BESTs)

BESTs were introduced in December 2002, as part of a national scheme for raising standards of behaviour and attendance in schools. These are multi-agency teams, that work in targeted areas to try to identify and support those whose attendance and/or behaviour is likely to cause problems. Most teams have four or five members of staff, such as:

- Educational and/or clinical psychologists

- Education welfare officers

- Behaviour support staff

- Speech and language therapists

- Health visitors,

- School nurses

- Primary mental health workers

- Social workers or family workers

BESTs are another example of the different services coming together to meet children's needs more effectively.

An Extended Role for Primary Support Bases (PSBs)

In 1999, a new role was established for the EBD Units (as they were described at that time), as staff felt that they did not receive children at an early enough stage, but often after they had been out of school for up to 6 months. Assessment was long-winded and the pupils, their families and schools were suffering from the delay. A new post was created for the head teacher of one of the schools, so that he could coordinate and develop the role of the Units. Phil Hewett worked closely with the head teacher of a primary BESD school and with the head of a PRU for Key Stages 1 and 2, in developing this new service, so that it would complement existing provision.

As a result, the staffing at the PSBs was doubled, so that they now offer outreach support to keep pupils in their own schools. The Behaviour Support Team act as gatekeepers and decide which children should be allocated one of the extended roll places. Only if this fails to give them enough support are they given places at a PSB. BESD schools concentrate on those with the highest level of need.

This new way of working has meant that a town with the highest number of exclusions previously now has no children of primary school age being excluded.

Education Improvement Partnerships (EIPs)

The many ways in which schools have been working together has been given further impetus by the creation of Education Improvement Partnerships.

Education Improvement Partnerships (EIPs)

EIPs were formerly known as Foundation Partnerships. In the spring of 2005, the DfES brought out a prospectus itemising the ways in which schools in a geographical area could form links to address particular issues. An EIP must be inclusive of all the schools in the area and set out its aims in terms of:

- Raising attainment and improving behaviour and attendance

- The personalisation of provision

- Delivering the five outcomes of ECM in all schools and through childcare and extended services

EIPs are intended to build on existing partnerships rather than replace them.

In the prospectus for *Education Improvement Partnerships*, the move to extend the ways in which services are provided is clearly set out, as the following two extracts reveal:

> *Federations will be well placed to develop into EIPs, and a number of them already have contracts with their local authorities to deliver services.*
> *Page 4*

> *Where an EIP is commissioned to take on functions previously delivered by a local authority, that local authority will devolve appropriate funding to partnerships, to enable them to deliver those functions. This, too, would be set out in joint agreements.*
> *Page 7*

This comes back to the point made previously, that all types of schools, whether individually or as a group, may provide services to other schools.

Points to ponder

■ Does your school commission services from other schools or, if not, would you like it to do so?

■ Do you provide services to other schools and, if not, are there any services you would like to provide?

Centrally retained services

Despite the amount of delegation of money to schools from the centre, most local authorities retain some key services, as part of their duties as regards children and young people with SEN. In some authorities part or all of the former local education authorities' functions have been taken over by private sector partners, such as Serco, W.S. Atkins, Nord Anglia or CEA, but certain services must be available to schools.

Educational Psychology services are particularly important to schools, as Educational Psychologists (EPs) are crucial in helping schools identify the nature of children's difficulties. EPs play a key role in undertaking the statutory assessments that may lead to a child receiving a statement. One of the problems with the statementing procedures being so laborious, is that the process ties up so much of the time that EPs would otherwise be able to spend in supporting schools more generally. Changes in the way they are trained will involve a move from a one-year master's degree to a three-year doctorate. This could create an even more difficult situation in schools, as there will be a hiatus before newly trained EPs are available to work in schools.

Parent Partnership services are statutory services, but are encouraged to operate at arm's length from local authorities. However, most remain part of the local authority, though a minority are out-sourced from the voluntary sector. Most services are attached to a single authority, though some may cover a number of smaller authorities. Their roles and responsibilities are set out in the SEN Code of Practice 2001. Parent Partnership coordinators provide support and advice to parents of children with SEN. Their role includes giving accurate, unbiased information on the options available to parents when it comes to their child's education. They provide a point of contact and general help to parents in navigating the complexities of the school system.

SEN advisers and **SEN advisory teachers** may lead teams or be part of a larger team of advisers who support school improvement. Their role includes working with schools in general to help them develop inclusive practice. Some may advise on the ways to support particular children. Peripatetic or visiting teachers may also be part of these teams. Specialist peripatetic teachers attached to central services work with individual children in a variety of settings and with a variety of needs. They provide specialist advice and support, including delivering in-service training (INSET). They possess detailed knowledge of particular conditions, such as sensory, or physical impairment, or autistic spectrum disorders.

In some areas, there is a move towards creating multi-disciplinary teams, as the drive to integrate services accelerates. Below is an example of a centrally funded service in Rotherham, which has many component parts. Social services is included in the team, and protocols have been developed for working with the health service through Primary Care Trusts (PCTs).

Primary Care Trusts (PCTs)

PCTs were established in April 2002 to take control of local health care, with strategic health authorities being responsible for monitoring performance and standards. PCTs receive their budgets directly from the Department of Health (DH).

Rotherham's Integrated SEN and Disability Service

Since 2003, Peter Rennie, Head of SEN Support Services in Rotherham, has been working with colleagues to create an integrated SEN and Disability Service, which started to be implemented in December 2005. The Service is about to move, so that all the different services will be co-located under the same roof. The Integrated SEN and Disability Service includes:

■ A service for hearing impaired children

■ A service for visually impaired children

■ An autism and communication team

■ The children's disability social work team

■ Residential care settings (for respite care) and the attached outreach workers

Protocols for joint working have also been established with the PCT and service level agreements (SLAs) set up for:

■ a speech and language therapist working with the autism and communication team

■ a school nurse adviser

■ a moving and handling co-ordinator

Budgets for the component elements of the service have, where necessary, been disaggregated from larger budgets and will be either aligned or pooled from April 2007.

As well as being involved in running central services for many years, Peter Rennie helped to found SENSSA, the SEN Support Services Association.

SENSSA

Established at the beginning of the 1990s, SENSSA is an organisation for all those who work in support services. They join either as individuals or belong to a team that has corporate membership. Its members work in a variety of contexts, including Speech and Language Therapy Teams, ASD and Communication Teams, Behaviour Support Teams and Learning Difficulty Teams.

Some of its members also belong to other more specialist organisations, but value belonging to an umbrella organisation as well, particularly at a time when there is more cross-fertilisation of services.

Contacts: peter.rennie@rotherham.gov.uk byoung@wakefield.gov.uk

This chapter has provided just a glimpse of some of the many and increasingly varied ways in which support to schools is being delivered. Support services, by working across all types of schools, help schools to become more inclusive, and by delivering specialist help to individual pupils, are a vital element in the creation of a flexible range of provision. As the number of providers in the field increases and the range of their work takes on a multi-disciplinary aspect as well, it becomes ever more necessary for there to be a strategic overview of what is happening on the ground. Local authorities may have become commissioners, rather than the sole providers of services, but they are best placed to identify where services overlap, or where there are gaps which need to be filled.

Points to remember

There is a growing number of ways that schools are being supported in providing for pupils with SEN. There has been a substantial shift from local authorities providing services to their role becoming one where they commission services instead.

Special schools are expected to deliver outreach as part of their dual role, and are doing so in a number of ways. Mainstream schools are also beginning to provide a range of services.

While retaining some services centrally, local authorities have delegated much of the money for SEN support to schools, who have the option of buying in to the services they want.

Final thoughts

■ What centrally held services are available in your area?

■ What other services does your school use?

■ Are there gaps in the provision of SEN services?

■ Are there ways in which you feel SEN support services could be better coordinated?

 # Recommended reading

Department for Education and Skills (2005a) *Draft Standards for SEN Support and Outreach Services*. Downloadable from the DfES website.

Department for Education and Skills (2005b) *Education Improvement Partnerships: Local Collaboration for School Improvement and Better Service Delivery*. Nottingham: DfES Publications.

OFSTED (2005) *Inclusion: the impact of LEA support and outreach services*.

SPECIAL CHILDREN (October, 2003) *At Your Service: An Interview with Peter Rennie*. Birmingham: Questions Publishing.

CHAPTER 6

Creating a flexible continuum of provision

The concluding chapter of this book draws together some of the themes that have emerged, including how schools and services are changing in order to respond to:

- A more complex population of pupils with SEN

- The effects of both the inclusion and ECM agendas

Some points are made about the role of head teachers and leadership teams in moving forward their schools and services.

Finally, proposals are made as to what more needs to be achieved in order to ensure that a flexible range of provision is available to all pupils, regardless of where they live, or the nature of their special educational needs.

Adjusting to change

For some time now, schools have been living through a period of immense change, when every aspect of their work has been under close scrutiny. The demands and pressures on school leaders and their staff have been relentless. In this context, it is remarkable that the strands of change, that have been the focus of this book, have demonstrated that despite all the other pressures, schools are prepared, and indeed, more than willing, to adapt and alter what they do, if by doing so, they will improve the lives and life chances of some of their more vulnerable students.

This book has been concerned, firstly, with the changes resulting from the inclusion of pupils with SEN and the way forward outlined in the SEN Strategy. The case studies showed how schools of all types are adjusting to educating children with different and more complex needs, as well as how schools and services are working more closely together, in recognition of their joint responsibilities towards all children and young people with SEN. Secondly, it has looked at the introduction of Every Child Matters, which, with its focus on putting individual children and their families at the centre of service delivery, sits very comfortably alongside the personalised approach used by those who are concerned with pupils who have SEN.

Adjusting to changing populations

It was clear from the case studies that all schools, whether mainstream or special, have seen a change in the range and complexity of needs they are trying to support. Yet, the overall number of children being identified as having SEN would appear not to be increasing. Indeed, the most recent figure of 17.8 per cent is a drop from the 20 per cent that was used as a round figure at the time of the Warnock Report in 1978 and has been quoted frequently since. However, any figures are only a rough guide, given that there is no official yardstick for measuring who has SEN and who does not. For instance:

■ A child who stands out as having a greater difficulty in learning than his or her peers in one school, will not necessarily be seen in the same way in another school

■ As mainstream schools become more skilled at meeting the needs of pupils with milder difficulties, and as children with more complex needs arrive in these schools, staff may change their cut-off point for describing which pupils have SEN

■ The change in the SEN Code of Practice may also have an impact, as pupils on what was Stage I of the original Code (meaning they had to be identified and put on an SEN Register), no longer have to be listed

There has been a drop in the numbers attending special schools, from 2 per cent of the school population to 1.2 per cent, although numbers have stabilised in the last few years. This means that part of the reason mainstream schools are seeing more pupils with complex needs is that they are receiving some of the children who would previously have been educated in special schools. This partly accounts for why the population in special schools is changing as well. As their less complex children may now be in mainstream schools, some of those places will have been taken by pupils of increasing complexity. So, where does this newer population come from? One reason that came out of the case studies, was the increasing number of babies who survive after being born very prematurely, some of whom turn out to have very complex needs. Another reason would seem to be the growing number of children with co-existing disorders. For instance, whereas most pupils with a diagnosis of MLD will now be in their local schools, special schools are receiving a number of children whose moderate learning difficulties are exacerbated by behavioural difficulties, communication disorders, or a number of other combinations of conditions.

In all types of schools, the effects of more children coming from unsettled home lives was noted, which was sometimes compounded by coming from disadvantaged backgrounds. These circumstances exacerbated any learning difficulties they might have or, in some cases, may have served to create them. Another way in which the schools were similar was the rise in certain conditions, such as ASD, AD/HD, and all forms of challenging behaviour. No definitive explanation has yet been forthcoming for this increase, although there are likely to be several factors involved:

■ More accurate and earlier diagnosis. Autism, for instance, is more likely to be diagnosed as a separate condition, due to advances in understanding, and to be diagnosed at an earlier stage.

■ More conditions are recognised. At one time, for example, dyslexia was almost synonymous with specific learning difficulties. Now that dyspraxia, dysgraphia and dyscalculia are also recognised as other kinds of specific learning difficulty, this is no longer the case. Various syndromes have been labelled that were previously unheard of. The SEN continuum contains descriptions of difficulties that were unknown to previous generations.

- Any difficulties pupils may have are taken much more seriously. The different conditions are distinguished from each other and addressed. Dyspraxia, for instance, is the label for children who might previously have been described as just clumsy, and no particular notice taken of their difficulties. Some pupils now labelled AD/HD might have been described as very lively and lacking in concentration, rather than being seen as having a disorder.

This is not to say that these diagnoses are unnecessary or wrong, but that because more trouble is taken over assessing the nature of a child's difficulties, and as our knowledge of different conditions increases, a growing number of disorders are being recognised and named. Schools are responding to these changes by adding to what they can provide for pupils with SEN, in terms of:

- Trying out new approaches

- Increasing the range of resources, in terms of staffing, accommodation and equipment

- Adjusting the curriculum and the way it is delivered

- Placing an emphasis on the importance of continuing professional development

The case studies show there is a growing range of provision available within mainstream schools, for instance, in the form of sensory rooms, 'time out' facilities or being resourced to cater for particular needs. In addition, there is a growth of offsite provision in the form of PRUs, which are extending the range of what they can offer, as well as linking more closely with other forms of provision. Special schools have adapted to their more complex population by creating different streams, departments or facilities within their schools. This has also been helpful in making more appropriate provision in schools covering a very wide age range, or where the school has become more generic and wants to make sure the right sort of support is being given to different groups of pupils within the school.

Increasing contact between the sectors

Whatever the reasons for the complexity of needs apparent in today's classrooms, schools are being presented with fresh challenges as they strive to provide for the whole gamut of needs, from global to specific learning difficulties and from disaffection to mental health problems. There is no clear dividing line between a child who is on the SEN continuum and one who is not, any more than there can be a clear cut-off point to determine who should be in a special school. That is why it is so important to have as much contact as possible between those working in different types of provision, and a flexible system within which the provision made can be adjusted to meet a child's changing needs.

One of the many encouraging themes to emerge from the case studies was the amount of contact that now exists between all parts of the education service, whether through co-locations and federations, partnerships or informal collaborations. All the schools in the case studies had established links with schools in the other sector, providing a form of professional development that cannot be overestimated, as well as opening up opportunities for an exchange of pupils as appropriate. In October 2004, Ofsted's report, *Special Educational Needs and Disability: Towards inclusive schools* had this to say:

> *Effective partnership work between mainstream schools and special schools on curriculum and teaching is the exception rather than the rule.*
>
> *(Ofsted, 2004: Main Findings, page 5)*

> *[...]*

> *Mainstream and special schools are still too isolated from one another; they are not providing the necessary expertise to ensure staff in mainstream schools are able to develop a coherent approach to inclusive education. (Ofsted, 2004: 23, paragraph 110)*

This shows how much things seem to have changed in the last two or three years, particularly in the outward-looking schools exemplified by the case studies, and in many other schools like them, which are forging links in a number of different ways. Although some of these links have been created by informal contact between schools in response to trying to address individual needs, the move towards greater collaboration has been enhanced by the development of federations and partnerships, as well as the move to co-locate schools. All these different types of links have meant that great strides have been taken towards making all schools feel they are part of the same education system, rather than isolated entities within it, and that they share responsibility for the progress and well-being of their pupils, including those who have SEN.

Deciding where pupils are placed

In the 2004 report by Ofsted, there is a comment about a child with PMLD in a mainstream school, and how the school was trying to meet her needs:

> *In one primary school, a pupil with profound and multiple learning difficulties was taught for most of each day by a teaching assistant on her own as there were no other pupils with similar needs and the mainstream lessons were unsuitable. The school did find some opportunities in music and art to include her with her peers, but, overall, she had a lonely experience each day. (Ofsted, 2004: 17, paragraph 74)*

It is not clear whether the Ofsted inspectors were thinking the school should have done more to accommodate her, or whether they were pointing out that it was inappropriate for the pupil to be in that setting, but there is a limit to how far a curriculum designed for the majority of pupils in a school can be made appropriate for a child who is likely to remain working at well below Level 1 of the National Curriculum (P Levels 1–3 is considered to be the range for most pupils with PMLD) for much or all of their school careers. Another way of looking at the situation is to ask these questions:

- Was the child being included in the life of the school?

- If not, could the school have done any more to include her?

- Was there another setting where she would have felt more included?

This goes back to the points made about inclusion in the opening chapter. All schools may or may not be inclusive schools. It is not a question of whether the school is a mainstream school or a special school, but of whether all its pupils feel equally included. Some children are happy to be different, they enjoy standing out in a crowd and receiving extra attention because their special needs are very apparent. Others hate being the only one who cannot be understood because they have a phonological disorder, are fearful of not being able to keep up in class because of their learning difficulties, or long to be with others who have similar needs.

Before the Warnock Report, the tendency was to place children in special schools according to their category of need, so pupils with behavioural problems attended schools for the maladjusted, pupils with learning difficulties were sent to schools for the educationally subnormal, and so on. The Warnock committee, however, wanted a shift to looking at children in terms of their *individual* needs. Since then, while categories are still used, there has been a move to treat pupils much more on an individual basis. This is to be applauded, but it does mean there is no easy way of deciding what provision should be made for different pupils. Table 6.1 shows the most prevalent type of needs, in descending order, for the different categories of children who are at School Action Plus of the Code of Practice or have statements.

	School action plus (%)	Statements (%)
MLD	30	25
BESD	26	14
SpLD	17	9
SLCD	13	11
ASD	2	12

SpLD = Specific learning difficulties

SLCD = Speech, language and communication difficulties

From House of Commons Education and Skills Committee (2006): Volume 2, Memorandum submitted by the DfES, paragraph 44.

Table 6.1 Most prevalent types of needs of those at school action plus and those with statements

Figure 6.1, however, looks only at pupils with statements. As the note at the foot of the pie chart indicates, this information does not take account of the growing number of pupils whose complex needs mean they have a diagnosis of more than one condition. Looking at this information, it is clear how much things have changed. Deciding where children should go to school on the grounds of the label they have, would take no account of co-existing disorders, but only of the main presenting needs, which in some cases is hard to determine. The fact that most conditions will have their own continuum from mild to severe would also be ignored. For instance, those with sensory impairments who are at one end of the spectrum, may have a slight loss of hearing or sight, while at the other extreme will be those who are totally deaf or blind.

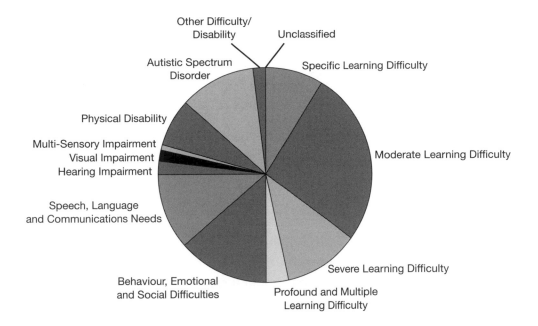

Other Difficulty/
Disability

Unclassified

Autistic Spectrum
Disorder

Specific Learning Difficulty

Physical Disability

Multi-Sensory Impairment
Visual Impairment
Hearing Impairment

Moderate Learning Difficulty

Speech, Language
and Communications Needs

Behaviour, Emotional
and Social Difficulties

Profound and Multiple
Learning Difficulty

Severe Learning Difficulty

Since data collection on type of need is relatively new, it needs to be interpreted cautiously. The Department is currently reviewing and refining the guidance given to schools on assigning primary and secondary types of need when they make their data returns.

Figure 6.1 Maintained primary and secondary schools and special schools: number of pupils with a statement of SEN by primary type of need – January 2005. From House of Commons Education and Skills Committee (2006), Volume 2, Memorandum submitted by the DfES, paragraph 44

In the pie chart above, each separate label has a continuum from mild to severe, apart from the ones representing global learning difficulties, which form their own continuum: MLD ⟶ SLD ⟶ PMLD. This may be one of the few cases where the label may be helpful in suggesting an appropriate setting, at least as far as pupils with SLD and PMLD are concerned. It is very hard for mainstream schools to make provision for children with very limited cognitive ability and to make them feel fully included in that setting, because of the ability gap between them and their peers (as illustrated by the pupil with PMLD mentioned in the Ofsted report). Any of the other labels, for instance ASD, will not, on its own, separate out those at the more extreme end of the ASD continuum, who are likely to have severe learning difficulties in addition to being classically autistic, and those who are only mildly affected, or have Asperger's syndrome.

While it may not be productive to try to find a mechanism for saying which of the 1.2 per cent of the school population should have places in special schools, it is clear that the vast majority can have their needs met in mainstream schools, some of them in resourced provision there, and that, at the other extreme, there are pupils, like those with the most limited cognitive ability, the most severely autistic, or those with the most challenging behaviour, who will be able to be more included in a special school, where the environment and everything in it, has been adapted to their particular needs.

In any case, in addition to knowing the type and severity of need, other factors that should come into play in determining placements include:

- Whether the child has co-existing disorders, for example, MLD and BESD, or PD and MSI

- Whether the child is socially well-adjusted and is confident, or has very low self-esteem

- Whether there is good support from the family, or a lack of a stable home environment

- Whether the child enjoys the attention created by having SEN or feels more included when in the company of others who have similar needs

The main question to consider in all this is: where will this particular individual be able to be most fully included in the life of the school community and how can his or her inclusion be achieved? When that question can be answered, and it can only be done on an individual basis, the way forward for that child becomes clearer. As has been said before, for the vast majority of pupils with SEN, this will be considering the type of support he or she will need within a mainstream classroom. For a smaller percentage, it may mean transferring to a different setting, where it is easier to adapt what is offered to the needs of that child, whether that turns out to be a resourced mainstream school, a PRU or a special school environment.

Making better use of specialist provision

Although there is a lot of talk about the importance of early intervention, the rhetoric is not always matched by the reality of what is actually happening in the lives of children and young people with SEN. While individual schools are often quick to spot difficulties and try to intervene early, there is a tendency to wait until pupils have fulfilled certain criteria before intervention from outside the school takes place. Head teachers of special schools, for instance, hear only too often from parents who will say: 'My child has now failed badly enough to come to your school. How soon can he or she start?' It has been a disappointment to many, for instance those working in MLD schools, that they are able to return far fewer pupils to mainstream education, than used to be the case, because only the more complex are being admitted in the first place. The 'revolving door' approach only works if pupils whose needs are not the most complex, are also able to be given places. If specialist provision, of whatever kind, is seen as a first port of call, rather than as a last resort when all else has failed, it would take some of the pressure off mainstream classes, address the *long tail of underachievement* that is holding back school improvement, and, most importantly of all, save pupils and their families from a great deal of stress. Students with SEN, whatever the nature of their difficulties, take up an undue proportion of staff time and energy. Allowing them quicker access to specialist provision, of the type that is most appropriate to their needs, would be the best way of raising standards for them and for the pupils with whom they are educated. Early intervention is cost effective in the long term and enables most pupils to spend more of their education in mainstream classes.

It should be one of the advantages of a more flexible continuum of provision that pupils (and staff) can move more freely in and out of what are presently discrete sectors on a short-term, part-time, or dual-role basis. Securing a range of provision in all areas should turn early intervention into more of a reality and free up all types of provision to more flexible use. There should be no need to continue to argue about the percentages of who should be in special schools, but of viewing all schools as part of the same system.

Creating greater flexibility in a system that moves away from the idea of different sectors to include all schools and the pupils within them could mean:

- Having pre-school assessment places in a range of settings, in order to make sure children start in the right environment on reaching statutory school age and no time is wasted in meeting their needs

- Providing short-term placements as another early intervention measure for those who show signs of distress, are starting to fall behind, or through their behaviour, begin to affect the progress of their peers

- Making part-time or dual-role placements a routine part of the role of specialist provision

The provision of outreach services

As well as the increasing contact that is clearly being established between special and mainstream schools in a number of formal and more informal ways, another change for the special schools that were not already providing an outreach service, has been the move to make this the other aspect of their dual role. Increasingly this work is being seen as one of the many types of support services available to schools and it can take many forms. Some examples were given in the case studies of schools and in the last chapter. This is a very positive development in bringing mainstream and special schools closer together and in securing the long-term future of special schools. Outreach work is never a one-way process; all schools have much to learn from each other and to contribute to each other's development. Increasingly, as has been noted, mainstream schools themselves are beginning to build up expertise in certain areas of SEN and to share it with other schools. There should be no feeling of competition either between schools, or between schools and other devolved and central services. More diverse school populations means that there is a need for a wider range of expertise to help schools understand how best to accommodate needs that are outside their experience, or where they feel the need to acquire more in-depth understanding of certain conditions, in order to provide the most appropriate forms of support.

Bringing about the ECM agenda

As well as contributing to the development of an inclusive service, schools have been finding ways of responding to the ECM agenda, so that it is incorporated into all aspects of a school's work. Staff who work closely with children and young people who have SEN, are more likely to have links with personnel from social services and from the health service. Schools are working with a wider range of professionals, who are either on the staff, or come in specially to offer help, so that children can receive targeted support. Some of the case studies showed this kind of support being offered to families as well. At local authority level, structures are being put in place, through the creation of children's services departments and children's trusts, to establish the framework for this newer way of working. There has been less impact at school level, although the development of children's centres is showing one way of providing coordinated services, by giving families access to education, health and social services all on one site. As the extended school provision begins to unfold, in the sense of schools being centres where a wider range of services will be made available, it will again help to deliver a more cohesive service to families and make it easier for them to access the services they need to support them. While these massive changes are still fairly new, already there is a greater appreciation of the contribution made by the different services, a willingness to work together in a more productive manner and to understand the sense in placing children and their families at the centre of what the services provide for them. Support services, too, are beginning to be multi-professional in their composition.

The other aspect of extended schools is the move to go beyond the usual pattern of school days and terms, in order to offer a wider range of services and activities. Again, children's centres are at the forefront of making this happen, but all the schools in the case studies were moving in this direction, opening up their schools to the wider community and being open for longer hours. Although the arrangements for extended schools are not due to be fully in place until 2010, considerable progress has been made already by schools of all descriptions.

The five outcomes of ECM and their relevance to inclusion

The five outcomes are providing a useful yardstick by which schools and services are able to measure the effectiveness of their work. Although meeting these outcomes may always have been part of the work of those who are concerned with the development of children and young people, they are now being considered in a much more overt way. Some of the case studies provided different examples of how the five outcomes are being embedded in all aspects of the life of a school.

For those working with children and young people with SEN, the five outcomes have a particular resonance, and could, indeed, be used to clarify the kind of support children need. At the moment, placement panels, which may include people who only know a pupil from reading the pile of paperwork in front of them, could be replaced by professionals from across the services, who know the child best, and this would obviously include the parents. What is now a paper exercise could become a mechanism for the pooling of knowledge to address these questions:

- What provision is necessary to maximise this child's *mental and physical health*?

- How can we help this child *feel safe* from bullying or being placed under undue pressure?

- What circumstances are necessary to ensure this child *enjoys his or her education* and therefore has the greatest chance of *making a success* of it?

- How can we help to give him or her the chance of *contributing positively* to the life of the school and to have a sense of belonging?

- Where will he or she have the best chance of learning the skills he or she will need to *achieve a productive life*?

Leaders of inclusive schools

It was very noticeable that head teachers, SENCOs and other members of the leadership teams, regardless of the type of school or service they worked in, had certain characteristics in common. These included:

- An enthusiastic and optimistic approach to the role, even when dealing with pupils who could be emotionally draining or relentlessly demanding

- An ability to seize opportunities to develop their schools or services, despite the pressures of keeping on top of the workload that accumulates each day

- A determination to improve what the school or service could offer and never standing still, or being satisfied with the status quo, however outstanding others judged the school or service to be

- Having a sense of what was over the horizon and the direction they needed to take in order to grasp opportunities and to be ahead of the game

- An ability to look outwards from their base and to be part of other networks, often at both local and national level

- Having an unquenchable thirst for knowledge, regardless of how much they knew already, and a willingness to share that knowledge with others

- Seeing their school or service in the context of the locality and reaching out to take joint responsibility for pupils with SEN wherever they were being educated

However long they had been in the job, these were leaders who continued to take an immense pride in their work and who were generous in sharing what they were doing with others. They had no conception of resting on their laurels, but only of moving forward, and using every day to find fresh ways of helping those who find it hardest to learn, to overcome the difficulties that stand in their way.

Towards the future

The 2006 Ofsted report identified three characteristics of effective provision for pupils with SEN:

1 Academic and vocational achievement

2 Personal development, including increasing independence and ability to organise themselves

3 Social development, including pupils' relationships and behaviour in a variety of situations

These features apply equally across all types of provision. The inspectors also mentioned the need for schools to have an inclusive ethos. As mentioned throughout this book, any type of school may or may not be inclusive. The future is to talk less (and, preferably, not at all) about the need to include all pupils in mainstream schools and, instead, build on the innovative work that is being done to make sure schools and services work together to create an education service that includes all its schools, and all the pupils within those schools.

The next step is to ensure that all local authorities maintain, or give their pupils access to, a similar range of provision. This should include mainstream schools that welcome all students who can be helped to access a mainstream curriculum, resourced provision in all its various forms, including on-site units, off-site units such as PRUs, and special schools that concentrate on particular types of need. All these schools should be able to draw on a range of services beyond the school.

Finally, the whole range of provision needs to be used more flexibly, so that needs can be addressed as soon as they arise or are identified, and one of a number of options can be considered, including short-term, part-time and dual-role placements in different settings.

As to the terminology of special educational needs, or SEN and disability, they have been enshrined in law, but for practical purpose, if every child not only matters, but matters equally, every child's individual interests, aptitudes and abilities need to be taken into account. In the same way that the barriers between schools are breaking down, hopefully to the point where it is no longer necessary to talk in terms of different sectors, the point should be reached where every child is special or different, and although some will continue to need a higher level of care and attention, this should be provided without necessarily having to talk about them as a separate category.

The inclusion and ECM agendas sit very comfortably together and should provide a clear direction for future work. The future is about personalisation, not about testing all children on the same day, regardless of whether or not it is setting them up for failure; it is about understanding the needs of the individual and where and how they can best be met, not about arguing about the right of special schools to exist; and it is about making sure that all children know that they matter, that they matter equally, and that they are entitled to receive the education that, for them, will deliver the five outcomes.

Final thoughts

■ Are you aware of pupils in your school or service who have co-existing conditions? If so, do you think this is because identification has improved, or the nature of children's difficulties has changed?

■ How do you think decisions should be made about the level of support pupils need and, if relevant, where pupils should receive their education?

■ What else do you think needs to be done in your area to ensure that there is a flexible range of provision? If it were all in place, would there still be a need for pupils to be educated outside your area? If so, who would this provision be for?

■ As Every Child Matters and personalised learning are being encouraged as a way of responding to the different aptitudes, abilities and interests of all pupils, do you think that it is necessary to retain the term 'special educational needs'?

Recommended Reading

Government Response to the Education and Skills Committee Report on Special Education Needs (October 2006). The Stationery Office.

House of Commons Education and Skills Committee (2006) *Special Educational Needs: Third Report of Session 2005–06, Volumes 1–3*. The House of Commons, London.

Ofsted Report (October 2004) *Special educational needs and disability: towards inclusive schools*.

# ME AND MY FRIEND LUCY

Lucy and me
Do a lot together,
And I know
We'll be friends for ever.

We walk around the playground
Talking to each other,
Stay away from the football,
And my little brother!

We tell all our secrets
With our other mates,
And every day we meet
Up at the school gates.

There's one thing I haven't mentioned,
My friend Lucy cannot walk,
She's no different from you and me
Even though Lucy cannot talk.

We have a lot of fun together
Every sie day,
Our school is called 'inclusive',
Lucy and me, like it that way.

Bethany Jagger, 8 years old
Whitfield and Aspen School Whitfield, Dover

'Like everyone else . . .' A collection of
poems on 'inclusion', NASEN 2006.

GLOSSARY

AD/HD	Attention deficit/hyperactivity disorder
ASD	Autistic spectrum disorder
BESD	Behavioural, emotional and social difficulties, (sometime referred to as SEBD or BSED)
BEST	Behaviour and education support teams
CAMHS	Child and adolescent mental health team
CDC	Child Development Centre
CSCI	Commission for social care inspection
DfEE	Department for Education and Employment
DfES	Department for Education and Skills
EAL	English as an additional language
ECM	Every Child Matters
EP	Educational psychologist
ERA	Education reform act
HI	Hearing impairment
HMCI	Her Majesty's Chief Inspector (of schools)
KS	Key stage
LA	Local authority
LDD	Learning difficulties and disabilities
LEA	Local education authority
LMS	Local management of schools
LMSS	Local management of special schools
LSU	Learning support unit
MLD	Moderate learning difficulties
MSI	Multi-sensory impairment
NAHT	National Association of Head Teachers
NASEN	National Association of Special Educational Needs
NMISS	Non-maintained and independent special schools
Ofsted	Office for standards in education
PCTs	Primary Care Trusts
PD	Physical difficulties/disabilities
PMLD	Profound and multiple learning difficulties
PNI	Physical and neurological impairment
PRU	Pupil referral unit
PSHCE	Personal, social, health and citizenship education
SEBD	See BESD
SEN	Special Educational Needs
SENDA	Special educational needs and disability act
SENSSA	Special educational needs support services association
SLAs	Service level agreements
SLD	Severe learning difficulties
TEACCH	Treatment and education of autistic and communication handicapped children
VI	Visual impairment

REFERENCES

Audit Commission (2002) *Statutory Assessment and Statements of SEN: In Need of Review?* Wetherby: Audit Commission.

Audit Comission (2007) *Out of authority placements for special educational needs.* Wetherby: Audit Commission.

Cheminais, R. (2003) *Closing the Inclusion Gap: Special and Mainstream Schools Working in Partnership.* London: David Fulton.

Department for Education and Science (1970) Education Act. London: HMSO.

Department for Education and Science (1981) Education Act. London: HMSO.

Department for Education and Employment (1994) Code of Practice on the Identification and Assessment of Special Educational Needs. London: HMSO.

Department for Education and Employment (2000) The Role of the local Education Authority in School Education. Nottingham: DfEE Publications.

Department for Education and Skills (2001a) Special Educational Needs and Disability Act. Nottingham: DfES Publications.

Department for Education and Skills (2001b) *Special Educational Needs Code of Practice.* Nottingham: DfES Publications.

Department for Education and Skills (2003a) *The Report of the Special Schools Working Group.* Nottingham: DfES Publications.

Department for Education and Skills (2003b) *Every Child Matters.* London: The Stationery Office.

Department for Education and Skills (2004a) *Removing Barriers to Achievement: The Government's Strategy for SEN.* Nottingham: DfES Publications.

Department for Education and Skills (2004b) *Every Child Matters: next steps,* Nottingham: DfES Publications.

Department for Education and Skills (2004c) *Every Child Matters: change for children in schools,* Nottingham: DfES Publications.

Department for Education and Skills (2004d) *The Children Act.* Norwich: HMSO.

Department for Education and Skills (2005a) *Draft Standards for SEN Support and Outreach Services.* Downloadable from www.dfes.gov.uk/consultations.

Department for Education and Skills (2005b) *Education Improvement Partnerships: Local Collaboration for School Improvement and Better Service Delivery.* Nottingham: DfES Publications.

Department for Education and Skills (2005c) *Higher Standards, Better Schools for All.* Norwich: The Stationery Office.

Department for Education and Skills (2005d) *Youth Matters.* Norwich: HMSO.

Department for Education and Skills (2006a) *Common Assessment Framework for Children and Young People: Managers' guide.* Nottingham: DfES Publications.

Department for Education and Skills (2006b) *Common Assessment Framework for Children and Young People: Practitioners' guide.* Nottingham: DfES Publications.

Department for Education and Skills (2006c) *National Audit of Support, Services and Provision for Children with Low Incidence Needs: Research Report 729.* Nottingham: DfES Publications.

Department for Education and Skills (2006d) *The Education and Inspections Act.* Norwich: HMSO.

Disability Rights Commission (2002) *Code of Practice for Schools: Disability Discrimination Act 1995, Part 4.* London: Disability Rights Commission.

Farrell, M. (2006) *Celebrating the Special School*. London: David Fulton.

Gibson, S. and Blandford, S. (2005) *Managing Special Educational Needs*. London: Paul Chapman Publishing.

Government Response to the Education and Skills Committee Report on Special Educational Needs (2006) Norwich: The Stationery Office.

Hayward, A. (2006) *Making Inclusion Happen: A Practical Guide*. London: Paul Chapman Publishing.

House of Commons Education and Skills Committee (2006) *Special Educational Needs: Third Report of Session 2005–06, Volumes 1–3*. London: The House of Commons.

Jordan, R., Jones, G. and Murray, D. (1998) *Educational Interventions for Children with Autism: A Literature Review of Recent and Current Research*. London: DfEE.

National Association of Special Educational Needs (2006) 'Like everyone else . . .' A collection of poems on 'inclusion' Tamworth: NASEN

Ofsted (2003) *Special Educational Needs in the Mainstream*. Downloadable from www.ofsted.gov.uk.

Ofsted (2004) *Special Educational Needs and Disability: Towards Inclusive Schools*. Downloadable from www.ofsted.gov.uk.

Ofsted (2005) *Inclusion: The Impact of LEA Support and Outreach services*. Downloadable from www.ofsted.gov.uk.

Ofsted (2006) *Inclusion: Does it Matter Where Pupils are Taught? Provision and Outcomes in Different Settings for Pupils with Learning Difficulties and Disabilities*. Downloadable from www.ofsted.gov.uk.

Palmer, S. (2006) *Toxic Childhood*. London: Orion.

Special Children (October, 2003) *At Your Service: An Interview with Peter Rennie*. Birmingham: Questions Publishing.

The Treasury (2004) *Choice for Parents, the Best Start for Children: a Ten-Year Strategy for Childcare*. Norwich: HMSO.

Tutt, R. and Barthorpe, T. (2006) *All Inclusive? Moving Beyond the SEN Inclusion Debate*. Devon: The Iris Press.

Warnock, M. (1978) *Report of the Committee of Enquiry into the Education of Handicapped Children and Young People*. London: HMSO.

Warnock, M. (2005) *Special Educational Needs: A New Look*. No.11 in a series of policy discussions. UK: Philosophy of Education Society.

INDEX